Act Two

Edited by David Self and
Ray Speakman

Hutchinson of London

Other drama anthologies published by Hutchinson, edited by
Alan Durband

New Directions
Dylan Thomas, N. F. Simpson, Eugene Ionesco, James Saunders,
David Campton

Playbill One
Beverley Cross, Alan Ayckbourn, David Cregan, David Campton,
Donald Howarth

Playbill Two
Ann Jellicoe, David Perry, Stewart Conn, David Shellan, Tom
Stoppard

Playbill Three
Alan Plater, John Mortimer, Alan Gosling, Ray Jenkins, Ronald
Duncan

Second Playbill One
Willy Russell, John Kershaw, David Shellan, Ken Taylor, Terry
Phillips and Jackie Girling

Second Playbill Two
Cecil Taylor, Gaie Houston, Doris Lessing, Derek Bowskill,
Charles Savage

Second Playbill Three
Don Shaw, Charles Wood, Charles Dyer, David Selbourne,
Henry Livings.

Prompt One
Alan England, Cecil Taylor, Trevor Harvey, Michael Barwis,
C.G. Bond

Prompt Two
Barry Hines, Peter Terson, Bob Taylor, David Rudkin, Don Shaw

Prompt Three
E. A. Whitehead, Roy Minton, Willis Hall, Robert Holles, John
Hale

Contents

Hutchinson & Co. (Publishers) Ltd
3 Fitzroy Square, London W1P 6JD

London Melbourne Sydney Auckland
Wellington Johannesburg and agencies
throughout the world

First published 1979
This selection and notes © David Self and
Ray Speakman 1979

Set in IBM Press Roman

Printed in Great Britain by the Anchor Press Ltd
and bound by Wm Brendon & Son Ltd,
both of Tiptree, Essex

1. Children's plays, English   2. English drama —
20th century
I. Self, David   II. Speakman, Ray
822′.9′1408   PN6120.A4

ISBN 0 09 136591 0

Introduction

Two of the four new plays published in this collection were written to form a double bill for staging by the National Youth Theatre in 1977; the other two plays were originally written for television.

Of these, the first, *Two Men from Derby*, is by the Yorkshire writer, Barry Hines, who is famous for such novels as *Kes* (*A Kestrel for a Knave*) and *The Blinder* (a story about a sixth former who has to make the decision between going to college or signing for a first division football club). *Two Men from Derby* is set in 1930 in a suburb of Sheffield and was based on an incident in the life of the author's grandfather, who was approached by Leicester FC to become a professional footballer.

Dick, the play's central character, never appears on stage. He is a young coal-miner and a gifted footballer, and the play is about the visit to his home of two officials from Derby County FC who are interested in signing him up as a professional player. However, he does not come home at the arranged time to meet them, even though he knew they would be coming. We are deliberately left in doubt whether this is because he has forgotten, or because he has gone to visit his mother who is seriously ill, or whether it is because he wants to avoid having to make the decision. It is quite clear that he enjoys football at an amateur level, where he does not have to try too hard, and that he enjoys his visits to the local pub with his mates.

But instead of seeing the situation through Dick's eyes, the leading character in the play is his young wife, Freda. They have been married for seven months and she is expecting a baby. Even compared with Dick's work down the pit, her life is hard. Indeed, she scarcely stops work throughout the play — existing only to make sure that all is ready for her man when he chooses to return from the pit or the pub.

Gradually, through her conversation with the two officials, we are subtly told a lot about Dick, but we also see how important his signing for Derby would be for Freda. For her it would mean an escape from an endless routine of drudgery. One of the men points out to her that she is better off washing pit clothes than wearing them and working down the pit, but her answer is that (unlike her) when the miner has finished his shift, he has finished for the day.

She sends out her neighbour's young son to look for her husband, but he cannot be found and the two men have to leave to catch a bus to begin their journey back to Derby. They have found out enough about Dick's character not to want to see him another day, and Freda knows she is condemned to a life of drudgery. She vents her anger on Dick's supper and his football boots, but her temper changes to submission, and she carries on with her work.

With its realistic and natural dialogue, it presents a sympathetic and moving picture of a young wife, her brief hopes of escape and her disillusionment. Trapped partly by the social conventions of the time and place (that a wife should be little more than her husband's servant), she suffers from Dick's selfishness.

However, the arguments are not weighted totally in her favour — it is also possible to sympathize with the hard-working miner who wants only to relax after his work underground, and who wishes to keep football as a relaxation and not to change it into work.

The play raises many questions about the role of women in society, about the use of 'free' time, about ambition, about marriage, and the family. The other plays in this collection are also about family relationships.

Loyalties was commissioned from the prize-winning writer Peter McDougall by BBC School Television. It is set in a small town on the east coast of Scotland, a town that has been caught up in the North Sea oil industry, and it is about a boy's loyalty to a friend and how that loyalty is tested.

Onnie has become friendly with a man some ten years older than himself and his parents vigorously oppose this friendship: it is 'unsuitable'. Gallahar has been in trouble with the police. Onnie remains loyal to his friend, but he is more defensive when the local policeman asks him about the friendship. The truth is that in Gallahar's company, Onnie feels grown-up, and he tries to enter into Gallahar's hobby of pigeon-racing in order to strengthen the friendship. He also talks about his relationship with his father. Surprisingly, Gallahar points out there is 'nothing much wrong' with Onnie's father — something Onnie does not want to hear.

Late that evening, Onnie chances to follow a drunken oilman who is staggering home from the pub. Suddenly Gallahar appears: he has been lying in wait for the oilman. Without seeing Onnie, Gallahar beats up and robs the oilman. Having witnessed the incident, Onnie runs away, but he (in turn) has been observed by the policeman, Wylie. Wylie visits Onnie's parents, who are keen that he should use the incident to break the friendship. In the police station, Wylie tricks Onnie into making a full statement, but it is only when Onnie leaves the station that he realizes he has been tricked into a betrayal of his friend.

Onnie goes to Gallahar to explain and to excuse his sense of guilt, but Gallahar refuses to blame him. The friendship has been only one-way and Gallahar does not feel betrayed. Onnie realizes this eventually and expresses his disgust at Gallahar's attack on the oilman. He leaves him to his pigeons and re-establishes friendship with boys of his own age.

It is a powerful and tightly written play which says a lot about the nature of friendship and about loyalty — particularly when that loyalty comes into conflict with family loyalties or with the truth. Like many people of his age, Onnie needs a close friendship and is flattered and excited by an apparent friendship with an older person. However, the relationship has no significance for Gallahar, and the agony and confusion are all Onnie's.

Unlike *Two Men from Derby,* which (though originally a television play) works well on radio or on stage, *Loyalties* is a script written expressly for its medium. Coupled with this, the Scots dialect may make it seem a difficult and inaccessible play for many readers. However, because it does so accurately and vividly portray the conflicts that many young people experience, it is a play well worth tackling. Besides the many discussion points it raises, it provides an excellent example of a good television script and a chance to study the way a television play can be constructed out of dialogue and images. (Re-working the theme in another setting and for another medium could, however, also be a challenging and rewarding creative exercise.)

Some of the bonds and conflicts present in the family in *Loyalties* reappear in Peter Terson's double bill of stage plays, *Family Ties.* Written to be performed by the National Youth Theatre as part of their annual summer season, they neatly complement each other, but they are also quite independent of each other — they are, for example, about completely different families — and they can be read or performed separately if required.

In both plays, though, Peter Terson looks at the tensions (and loyalties) present in family ties, at the problems of children reaching adulthood, and at the tragicomic agony of being a parent. Unlike the case in Peter McDougall's play, the central character is not a teenager but the father of the family. We are asked to see things from his point of view.

But while *Wrong First Time* (the first of Terson's two plays) deals with the serious problems that can occur in a family, it is primarily a comedy; yet while some of the characters are little more than the comic caricatures we associate with farce, others are more 'normal' and therefore more sympathetic.

It begins with the father's somewhat cynical belief that 'Girls always marry the wrong man first time round'. His belief is fuelled by his two elder daughters, already married. Emily has married Claude, an empty-headed Adonis who does little but inspect himself in the mirror while Emily dedicates herself to finding him a job worthy of his looks, but which requires no talent or ability. Sandra has married Smudge, a Hell's Angel, and finds herself married as much to a Yamaha 750 as to a man.

When Penny, the youngest daughter (who is still at school), brings home Barry, her boyfriend, he is greeted with sighs of relief. He is 'normal'; a likeable, respectable, hard-working sixth former with ambitions to become an architect. Perhaps Penny will disprove her father's theory. But only a little later Penny discovers she is pregnant, and the rest of the play is taken up with Barry's and her attempts to sort out their problems. Penny's easygoing working-class family is contrasted with Barry's comically pretentious parents; and in the light of Penny's problems, her sisters begin to question their own marriages.

It is an entertaining and amusing play, but also one that poses a number of quite serious questions about love, marriage and what brings (and keeps) young people together. Penny's decision in the final moments of the play especially will give rise to much discussion.

If Terson writes with much sympathy for the predicament of the young in *Wrong First Time,* in *Never Right, Yet Again* his sympathies are almost all on the side of Dad.

Duncan Stoner is a liberal-minded, long-suffering father. For years he has indulged and tolerated his children. He found a job for his selfish older son, Kirby, who now sees it is as little more than a place to 'knock things off from', and home as a place where you are fed and find clean shirts. Wendy, the daughter, is subject to moods and a series of infatuations; in a 'little-girl' way, she is over-fond of her father and has not established any relationship with a boy of her own age. Ian, the younger son, is a relentless clown, taking nothing seriously and making school and home into platforms for his jokes.

The three children see their father as a source of food, comfort and cash; not as a person. Their view of him is directly in conflict with his own view of himself; and, in conversation with his wife, we catch glimpses of this private, inner existence — a world of personal longings, passion and memories.

At a formal tea party to welcome Kirby's fiancée (and also in the presence of a college friend of Wendy's), Duncan is goaded further than he can stand by the banter of his children. In an explosion of truth, he asks them if they are so selfish they can see no further than his slippers and armchair. He goes on to tell his children they are the trivia of his life; he has hidden depths they have never imagined, they are only 'the emotional shallow-end' of his experience.

But while he has told them he has an inner life, he has not let them see it; and, as the children switch the record player on, there is a feeling that the outburst will be forgotten. 'We're good at hiding it', says Mum, as 'one more time' they put on a face for the sake of their children.

This is possibly a very cynical play. It is also a genuine and perceptive study of a parent who feels he is losing his identity and becoming 'only' a parent. It shatters the myth (believed by some young people) that the middle-aged are without passion or longings; and it is that modern rarity, a play that suggests that youth is callous and selfish, while the middle-aged can deserve our sympathy. Like *Wrong First Time* it is funny enough to be entertaining and, also like that play, it presents a strong challenge to any young readers and actors. Just a part of that challenge is outlined in the suggestions for follow-up activities beginning on page 166.

Notes on Presentation

Reading

Even the most informal classroom reading of a playscript is helped by rehearsal. Remember, not even the experienced professional actor is happy to sight-read, but usually prefers to have had the chance at least to look over his part before a first reading in front of his colleagues. So, once a play has been cast, those who will be reading should be given the chance to look over their lines, make sure they know where they enter and exit, that they know when to pause, when to 'come in quickly' at the end of the previous speech, and indeed that they appreciate the mood, etc., of their character at any given moment.

Note that (especially in the case of those plays with small casts) it is possible for a class to break up into small groups, and for each group to rehearse its own interpretation of the play, before one group presents its reading to the whole class.

Note too that it is much easier to read to a class from the front of a traditional classroom, and from a standing position or a position where you can be seen by your audience.

In preparing the scripts for inclusion in this book, we have selected the radio adaptation of *Two Men from Derby* rather than the original television version, as the former reads more effectively in the classroom. We have rewritten the stage directions in *Loyalties* so that when the play is being read aloud these directions (and, indeed, the directions in all four plays, along with the scene titles) can be read aloud by an 'announcer'. (In the classroom presentation, it might be helpful if he or she were in view of the audience but away from the acting area.)

Note that, provided these directions are read sympathetically, a television play like *Loyalties* will read as fluently in the classroom as will a radio or stage play; but it should not be forgotten that like any good television play, it was conceived in visual terms, and it will be fruitful to discuss (as the original director must have done) where and how each scene should be 'shot' to realize the author's intention. Indeed, as has been suggested, the juxtaposition of television and stage playscripts in this collection could lead to a study of the differing natures, possibilities, limitations and constructions of such plays.

Tape-recording

One way of presenting *Two Men from Derby* would be to record it on tape. If this is done, then the directions must be translated into sound effects or realized by the actors' movements, etc., as happened when it was produced for radio.

Loyalties could also be tape-recorded. If so, it will be necessary either to write in a part for a story-teller (or narrator), based on the stage directions; or to invent extra dialogue to make clear to the listener what is happening.

More ambitiously, it might prove possible to tape-record the dialogue and sound effects, and to take a number of 35 mm slides to illustrate the action, and so 'stage' the play as a 'tape-and-slide' presentation.

The following general points may be of help when tape-recording:

a   Discover the directional qualities of your microphone – that is, from how wide an angle it picks up sound.

b   Even the best microphone cannot produce a good recording over a long distance from the sound source. For speech, it should be 30–40 cm from the mouth. (Those readers with stronger voices can obviously be further away than those who do not project well.)

c   It is much easier to record a play with the actors standing rather than sitting. (They can then easily tiptoe away when not involved in a dialogue, and so allow those that are speaking to stand in the best position.)

d   Don't hold the script between mouth and microphone, and avoid rustling pages.

e   Rooms with bare walls are unsuitable for making recordings in, as they have a very echo-y sound. Where possible, use a carpeted, curtained room (unless of course an echo-y effect is required!).

f   It is possible to minimize echo (and also to lessen background noise) by speaking closer to the microphone and by turning down the recording level. When doing this, a better sound may be achieved by speaking across the microphone rather than directly into it.

g   Sound effects are important in creating a sense of location. Either they can be 'spot effects' created at the time of recording (e.g. doors opening and closing, cups of tea being poured, etc.) or recorded (either on another tape or from commercial discs). Don't worry about including every sound — concentrate on background noises which suggest location (e.g. the seashore, the street, etc.) and those sounds which indicate the arrival or departure of a character. Don't allow clumsy and accidentally comic sounds (like 'artificial' footsteps) to clutter or confuse the much more important dialogue.

h   Gently fading out the very last few words or sounds of a scene and fading in the first sounds of a new scene will suggest a transition from one scene to another.

Staging

Peter Terson's double bill was written to be staged by a youth company, and so the most natural and obvious response to the script is to produce it on stage — either informally to a small audience or in a more formal production with fully 'dressed' sets. (Both these plays, and also *Two Men from Derby*, gain much from being staged in credible and realistic settings, full of domestic detail.)

For *Wrong First Time* the stage should be divided into three areas. Stage right forms the Larson's living room; stage left the Bellamys' drawing-room; and in front of these two sets, ideally at a lower level, is Frank Larson's garden.

For *Never Right, Yet Again* the set shows the living room; in front of this (again ideally at a lower level) is Mr Stoner's garden.

Note that it should be possible to light just one of these areas at any time, and that the plays will be more effective the speedier are the transitions from scene to scene.

In their first production, both plays were cast from a youth company, and young people should not shrink from playing the parental roles. Indeed many insights could be gained by playing such parts. However it is worth considering whether the impact on an audience might be the greater if adults take the parental roles while the children are played by actors of a younger generation.

Though *Two Men from Derby* was originally a television play and is here represented by the radio version, because it all takes place in the one setting, it will transfer easily to the stage. Note one point which dominated the original television production: Freda works very hard throughout the play, and the fact that her life is a never-ending succession of chores must be obvious in any production.

Because *Loyalties* is a television script and requires a variety of outdoor locations, it will prove hard to present it on stage realistically (without major adaptation). It will work successfully, however, if it is given a stylized production either in the round or on an almost empty stage. Specially taken 35 mm slides or projected scenery can announce location to an audience, and the use of sound effects can be an effective substitute for scenery (especially in outdoor scenes such as those near the sea). In indoor scenes, the use of stage scenery should be severely restricted so as to preserve fluency and speed of staging. Part of the success of any television play lies in the fact that it can cut from one scene to another and also include scenes which involve travel (e.g. walking along a street). When a stage performance of a television play is undertaken, lighting changes must be used to effect such 'jump-cuts' and to make us believe the acting area now represents a different location.

NB Although all the plays in this series of volumes will stand on their own, double (and even triple) bills can be constructed to form a challenging evening's entertainment — possibly with the different years in a school each presenting one play.

Acknowledgements

For permission to publish the plays in this volume, the editors are grateful to the following authors and their agents: Barry Hines and Curtis Brown Ltd for *Two Men from Derby*; Peter McDougall and A.D. Peters & Co Ltd for *Loyalties*; Peter Terson and Harvey Unna & Stephen Durbridge Ltd for *Family Ties*.

Two Men from Derby

Barry Hines

Characters

Freda, wife of Dick Hayes, a coal-miner and amateur footballer; they have been married seven months, and she is expecting a baby

Joe } two officials of Derby County Football Club
George }

Winnie, Freda's next-door neighbour, an older woman
Stanley, Winnie's young son

First televised on BBC 1 on 21 February 1976 and subsequently broadcast on BBC Radio 4 on 23 October 1976

This text is that of the radio version, as adapted by the author from his television script

Two Men from Derby

Scene: **The kitchen of terraced house in the North of England, 1930.** *It is washday. In order to accommodate the washing tackle in the small room,* **Freda** *has had to move the furniture around to make the space of the hearth bigger. She has pushed the table back against the dresser and rolled the hearth rug back. The room is crowded and untidy and there are separate piles of clothes on the floor and on the table. The kitchen is hot and steamy. This is the equipment* **Freda** *is using for washing: two peggy tubs, a peggy legs, a rubbing board and a mangle. There is also a boiler working. This is set between the fireplace and the sink in the corner. There is also a clothes-horse near the fireplace.* **Freda** *takes a sheet out of a tub and puts it through the mangle. We hear the squeezed water draining back into the tub, and the cogs of the mangle as* **Freda** *turns the handle. It is hard work. She continues turning the handle.*

Freda: I shall have to go and get some oil for this mangle. I'm going to have arms on like a collier if I don't get it seen to.

[*There is a knock on the door*]

Wait a minute!

[*She finishes mangling the sheet, then goes to the door. She opens the door, and we hear the sound of rain*]

Joe: Does Dick Hayes live here?

Freda: [*Pause*] Yes. Why?

Joe: Is he in?

Freda: No. He's not come home yet. He's still at work.

Joe: Oh. [*Pause*] He said he was on nights this week. He said he'd be in.

Freda: He should have been, but he's swopped shifts. His mother's on her last legs and he didn't want to be at work in case owt happened to her in t'night.

Joe: Oh. I see. [*Pause*] What time are you expecting him home then?

Freda: [*Pause*] He shouldn't be long now. I've got his dinner on.

Joe: Can we wait for him then?

Freda: [*Pause*] What do you want him for, anyway?

Joe: We're scouts for Derby County. I'm Joe Kenny and this is George Hirst. We want him to come to Derby for a trial.

Freda: Oh. You'd better come in then.

[*She lets them into the house and closes the door behind them. They knock the rain off their caps by banging them on their thighs, and shake the rain off their overcoats by unbuttoning them and shaking them*]

It's still raining then?

Joe: Raining? It's raining twice. It'd be a grand day for a funeral would this.

Freda: My heart dropped a mile when I saw you standing there. I thought you were from t'pit. I thought summat had happened to him.

Joe: Our hearts dropped a mile an'all when we got off that bus and they told us how far we'd to walk in this lot.

Freda: Which bus did you come on?

Joe: We caught one at Sheffield Land Top to Hoyland.

Freda: It's a fair walk from Hoyland, you must be worn out. Here, let me shift this basket and this pile of clothes so you can sit down.

[*Pause while she moves the washing basket and the pile of clothes from the chairs. The two men sit down*]

Joe: That's better. I was ready for a breather.

Freda: Does he know you're coming?

Joe: We had a word with him after the match at Thorpe on Saturday.

Freda: Oh, you went to Thorpe, did you?

Joe: We'd seen him play a few times before that though. We'd never let on who we were, though, just in case it put him off his game.

Freda: Do you think he's good enough to be a footballer? A professional footballer I mean?

George: He could be.

Joe: Oh, he's good enough. Don't you bother about that missus. He's a natural.

Freda: They all say that. They all say that he's a good player. His dad says that when he was three years old he could throw a ball up between his heels and catch it on his foot when it came down.

George: It's not music hall turns we're after. You need more than a bit of juggling to make the grade as a pro footballer.

Joe: He's a natural though, George. You've only see him running with the ball. It stands out a mile.

Freda: He takes after his dad they say. He was a centre forward as well.

Joe: It's often the case. Centre forwards are born, not made. Just like — scholars; and royalty.

[*She takes another sheet out of the tub and mangles it*]

Freda: He scores a lot of goals, don't he. Not that I know much about it. He never tells me owt. It's his dad who tells me. I go round and do a bit of cleaning up now that his mother's bad.

Joe: That's what we want him for. He's one of them players who'll score goals whatever league he plays in.

Freda: Excuse me, mister. But can I lend your chair a minute to hang these sheets up on the line?

Joe: Course you can. [*Pause*] Here you are.

Freda: I'll not be a minute. [*Then, hanging up the sheets*] I'm sorry it's not very comfortable. You couldn't have come on a worse day. But I'll have to get done. I can't have a house like a tip when Dick comes in. [*Pause*] That's it. You can have your chair back now.

Joe: Ta.

George: What time did you say he'd be back?

Freda: [*Pause*] He should be back any time now. I'm going to mix his puddings in a minute. Do you want a cup of tea while you're waiting? You must be frozen to the marrow if you've come all that way in this lot.

Joe: George?

George: [*Pause*] Go on then.

Joe: Right. Well, if it's not too much trouble, it'd come in very nicely, thank you.

Freda: The kettle's nearly boiled, I was just going to have a cup myself.

[*She pokes the fire to hurry the kettle up*]

Where is it anyway, Derby?

Joe: [*Studying*] It's about, forty miles from here I should say, wouldn't you, George?

George: Fifty'd be nearer the mark.

Freda: It's a fair stretch then isn't it? How do you get there?

Joe: From here? You walk it to Hoyland. Then you catch a bus to Sheffield Lane Top. From there you catch a tram to the station. Then you catch a train to Derby.

Freda: It's a right trek isn't it?

Joe: You've never been to Derby then?

[**Freda** *mashes the tea*]

Freda: Never been! I've only been to Sheffield twice and that was to see my mother in hospital. Once when she lost our Betty, and once when she had that growth removed from her neck. [*Pause*] Do you both want sugar?

Joe: Three for me please, missus. And you can put it in with a number five shovel if you've got one.

George: Just one for me. [*Pause*] That's enough.

[**Freda** *stirs both pots and hands them to the men*]

Freda: Here you are.

Joe: Just the job.

Freda: He never said you were coming.

George: We arranged it after the match. We didn't have time to talk because we'd a train to catch.

Freda: He never said owt when he got home. [*Pause*] He said that the centre half had been clogging him to death all game. His shins were black and blue when he washed his legs to go out on Saturday night.

Joe: Oh, gets some clog iron, there's no doubt about that.

Freda: [*Quietly, more to herself than to the men*] Mind you, he never does tell me owt. He's never in to tell me, is he?

Joe: He's got to expect it though, hasn't he. They're not going to stand there and let him run past 'em, are they?

Freda: His dad says he asks for it sometimes. He says he tries to make mugs of 'em. He says that he's got too much old buck.

Joe: Oh, he's cheeky all right.

George: Cocky. Cocky's the word.

Freda: I know. That's his trouble. [*Pause*] Clever Dick. That's what they used to call him at school. Nobody can tell him owt.

Joe: Nobody has to tell him how to get that ball into the back of the net, that is a certainty.

George: How old is your husband, Mrs Hayes?

Freda: Wait a minute, will you. I'd better mend the fire and get his puddings on.

[*She opens the pantry door. We hear her go down the cellar steps, then we hear the sound of shovelling and she comes back up the steps carrying a large shovelful of coal. She throws the coal on the fire and puts the shovel down in the hearth*]

Now then, what were you saying?

George: I said, how old is your husband?

[*Pause.* **Freda** *cracks two eggs into a basin and pours milk into it*]

Freda: Twenty-two. Just.

George: He must have been approached before by other clubs.

[**Freda** *beats the pudding mixture*]

I mean, it's not as though he's still a lad, or that nobody's ever seen him play. He's well known for miles around here. He's a marked man every time he steps out on to the field.

Joe: We couldn't believe it first time we saw him. We'd had these reports from our local scout: come up and see this Dick Hayes he kept saying. Come up and see him before its too late. He's another Steve Bloomer he said. Can you remember that dummy he sold that centre half, George? Talk about send a man the wrong way. He finished up amongst the supporters against them lav walls down the far side.

[**Freda** *opens the oven door and slides the pudding tins in*]

By, that smells good missus. What you cooking?

Freda: Same as I cook every Monday — hash.

[*She closes the oven door*]

George: He should have shot then though, instead of trying to dribble round the goalie.

Joe: It was only the mud that stopped him though, George. He was round the goalie. He'd have left him on a dry day.

George: But it wasn't a dry day. He was trying to do too much. He'd have scored with a shot.

Joe: He did get two, though, George. Be fair.

George: I know, but they lost didn't they?

Freda: [*Pause*] One or two blokes have been to see him. They used to go to his mother's an'all before we were married.

George: Where from?

Freda: Local clubs mainly, Sheffield, Barnsley, Huddersfield. He should have gone to Sheffield Wednesday once for a trial but he never got off.

George: Why?

Freda: He didn't get up in time and he missed the train. [*Pause*] That was when he was still living at home though.

[*She goes over to one of the tubs, and rubs clothing up and down the rubbing board*]

I wish he would go.

Joe: Go? Where?

Freda: Derby. Anywhere.

Joe: It's a good club. He'd be well looked after.

Freda: How much would he get paid?

George: He's late, isn't he, missus?

Freda: Just wait a minute will you?

[*She knocks three times on the wall which divides her kitchen from the next-door neighbour's kitchen*]

Hey, and I've forgotten to put his washing water on for him. You've fair put me out, calling unexpected like this.

[*She fills a pan from the tap and puts it on the gas. She lights a match and the gas pop as it lights. There is a knock on the door, then the door opens*]

Winnie: Do you want me, love?

Freda: Is your Stanley still off school, Winnie?

Winnie: Why, do you want him?

Freda: Will you ask him to run down to the Queen's for me and ask Ernest if Dick's there? If he is, will you tell him he's to come straight home, as there's two men from Derby come to see him?

Winnie: I'll send him straight away.

[**Winnie** *goes out closing the door behind her*]

Freda: He sometimes calls for a drink before he comes home.

Joe: You need one, I can tell you. I know, I've worked down there. [*Pause*] When I first started down the pit the pubs were open all day. Ilk Johnson who kept the Acorn used to be open when the night men came off at six. He used to have all the pints half-pulled on the bar, then start filling them up when he heard the clogs coming up the lane. [*Pause*] One morning he laid too long and wasn't up. We were all outside banging on the door and shouting. Joe Jones picked some muck up and threw it against the bedroom window. Hey up! he shouted. Are you stopping in bed all day then, or what? [*He laughs quietly to himself as he remembers it*] He was a bugger was Joe. He got crushed between two tubs.

Freda: He'll not be long. The Queen's only a cock stride away. You'll have passed it on t'corner on your way up.

George: I hope not. We've a train to catch at half past five.

[**Freda** *puts some clothes through the mangle. There is a quiet knocking on the door*]

Freda: That'll be Stanley. Come in, love!

[**Stanley** *opens the door and comes in*]

Is he there love?

Stanley: No, Mr Turner says he's gone.

Freda: Did he say where to?

Stanley: No, he just said he'd gone out.

Freda: [*Pause*] Well. Will you run to the Hare and Hounds for me then, love, and see if he's in there?

Stanley: All right.

[*He runs out of the house and bangs the door behind him*]

George: Noisy young bugger.

Freda: [*Calling after him*] Come straight back and tell me won't you Stanley? [*Then to the men*] He sometimes calls in the Hare and Hounds instead of the Queen's.

George: Does he sometimes call in them both?

Freda: [*Pause*] How much did you say he'd get paid?

Joe: It depends. At his age he'd probably start on about eight pounds a week. But if he stopped with the club and did well, after a few years he could be bringing home owt up to fifteen pounds with bonuses.

Freda: Fifteen pounds a week! Just for playing football?

Joe: Better than the pit isn't it, missus? How much is he getting there, three or four pounds a week?

Freda: I don't know. He don't tell me. He just gives me my house-keeping and keeps t'rest for himself.

Joe: Well it'll not be above five, I can tell you that. [*Pause*] Then there's a free house, of course, and he'd travel about a lot. . . .

Freda: A free house?

Joe: Rent-free I mean; well, nearly. A club house; we don't give it to you, I don't mean that.

Freda: What sort of house? What are they like inside?

Joe: What sort? I don't know. What sort of houses are they George?

[*George does not answer him.* **Joe** *is forced to carry on*]

Well. [*Pause*] Bigger than this. A bathroom. Nowt fancy mind. But nice; in town.

Freda: It sounds lovely.

Joe: Oh, they're looked after all right, are our players. It's a good club. It's got a good record. We were Division 1 runners-up 1895-6, and last season. Division 2 champions 1911-12,

1914-15, and runners-up in 1925-26. We've been FA Cup
finalists three times: 1898, 1899 and 1903. And we've had
some great players. There was the immortal Steve Bloomer of
course — old paleface — who played twenty times for England
and altogether scored 297 goals for Derby. Then there's Jack
Bowers, playing now. He looks as though he might even beat
Steve's individual total this season; he's got 27 goals already ....

Freda: [*Not listening, cutting him off*] It sounds lovely. I've
always wanted to live in a town.

Joe: Don't get carried away, missus. It wouldn't be Buckingham
Palace. We're not the Arsenal. Not yet anyway.

Freda: No, but it'd be better than this hole, wouldn't it?

[*There is no disputing this fact. But it would be insulting to
say so, so* **Joe Kenny** *keeps quiet*]

Owt'd be better than being stuck in here all day. And I
wouldn't be washing pit clothes any more would I? Look at
'em!

[*She throws them into the tub and we hear her viciously
using the peggy legs on them*]

Joe: You're better off washing 'em than wearing 'em, I can tell
you that. If you'd to go down there six days a week you'd be
thankful for what you've got. You're better off filling washing
tubs than coal tubs, believe me.

[*There is a knock on the door*]

Freda: Come in, Stanley!

[**Stanley** *comes in. He is panting this time*]

Is he there?

Stanley: No. They say he's not been in.

Freda: Has anybody seen him?

Stanley: I don't know. I didn't ask 'em all.

Freda: All right love. [*Pause*] Now then. If I give you a penny will you run to the Prince, The Star and the Club and ask there for me? [*Pause*] Do you know where they are?

Stanley: Club? I don't know where that is.

Freda: Down Fitzwilliam Street. That big red brick building near the bottom.

Stanley: Do you mean near where my uncle Walter lives? Where that bowling green is over their back wall?

Freda: That's it, love. Now then, tell me where you're going.

Stanley: [*Haltingly as he remembers the names*] Prince. Star. Club.

Freda: And what are you going to say?

Stanley: I'm going to say. Has anybody seen Mr Hayes? And if he's there, he's to come straight home 'cos there's two men to see him.

Freda: That's a good lad. Two men from Derby Football Club tell him.

Joe: Derby County Football Club.

Freda: Here's your penny.

[*There is a jingling of coins as* **Freda** *finds him a penny from her purse*]

Now off you go.

George: Wait a minute, lad. And there's another penny for you if you look sharp.

[*He places the coin on the table*]

Freda: Off you go now then, love.

[*He leaves the house. The door bangs behind him*]

[*Calling after him*] Don't be long will you, Stanley?

George: He'd better not be, or we'll have gone by the time he gets back.

Freda: Can't you catch a later train?

George: There isn't a later train. We've to be on that ten to four bus from Hoyland, or we'll miss it.

[**Freda** *starts to soap and rub the pit clothes viciously up and down the rubbing board*]

Freda: Men. You can't rely on 'em for two minutes together.

Joe: Well, judging by the look of you, you can rely on 'em for one thing, that is a certainty.

Freda: Ar, and that's about all.

Joe: Get away with you. You don't know you're born.

Freda: You what! Stuck in here all day washing and ironing and cooking and cleaning. Never going anywhere week in and week out. What sort of life do you call that?

Joe: And where do you think your husband goes every day, to a picnic? I know. I've worked down there. [*Pause*] I can remember when I was playing for Huddersfield and we looked like going down one year and I called in a pub that I used to go in before I left home. As soon as they saw me they were at it, having me on, making fun of me. How did we go on against such and such? How many goals had I let in against so and so? One bloke shouted across, you look like going down if you're not careful, Joe. Ar. I said, but even if we do it'll still be better than going down t'pit.

Freda: [*Pause*] I know, but at least when you've finished your shift, you've finished for the day. I've never done. Let alone my work, I'm doing Dick's mother's washing every week, and

I'm expecting a bairn in three months. And if everybody round here's owt to go by it'll not be the last either. It'll be the same old tale, stuck here for ever with a cart-load of kids growing up round me.

Joe: Everybody else has to put up with it.

Freda: *You* don't put up with it. My mother always said that if men and women had babies in turns and t'men had theirs first, there wouldn't be a family in this country bigger than two. [*Pause*] She was right an'all. What do men know about it? They bring their money home on a Friday and they think that's it. It's dinner, washed, changed and out. The next time you see 'em's either in bed stinking of beer, or next morning when they're shaking you awake to get up and get their breakfast.

Joe: A man's got to have some enjoyment when he's been at work all day. He'd go mad if he didn't.

Freda: And what about a woman? Don't she? Don't she work all day?

Joe: I know; but that's different. That's woman's work. A woman's used to it, isn't she?

Freda: A woman has to be, don't she? Look at Dick. He's a good husband. He works hard. I'm not staying owt about him. And don't think I don't know owt about t'pit, my dad and all five brothers were colliers and I was brought up with it. But we've only been married a few months and I hardly see owt of him already. [*Pause*] I don't know why men bother getting married, honestly. He sees more of his mates than he sees of me. He's swapped houses that's all. Instead of his mother feeding and seeing to him, I'm doing it instead.

Joe: What do you expect him to do when he comes home, just stop in all night?

Freda: *I* do.

Joe: I know you do. [*Exasperated now*] But that's different.

Freda: Why is it? Why don't he spend a bit more time with me, instead of wanting to be out boozing every night with his mates?

Joe: Because he needs to. When you've been down that hole all day you need to get out a bit. You need to get a few pints down you. They might be the last you'll get.

George: I think your puddings are done, missus.

[*Suitable exclamation from* **Freda**, *then she opens the oven door and takes the pudding tins out. There is a pause while she examines them*]

Freda: They're not too bad. They'll soften up when they get some gravy on 'em. [*Pause*] Where the hell is he? It's time he was home now.

Joe: They'll save a bit, won't they?

Freda: You know why he's late, don't you?

George: Why?

Freda: Because it's washday and it's raining. He hates coming home when t'house is all upset and there's washing hanging up everywhere.

Joe: You can't blame him for wanting a bit of comfort when he's been where he has for eight hours, can you?

Freda: No, and you can't blame me because this house isn't big enough to swing a cat round in, and I've nowhere else to hang things up. So he stops out drinking. Or he slopes off somewhere with one of his mates for an hour or two and leaves his dinner spoiling on the oven top.

Joe: It's a hard life.

Freda: You're not kidding mister. Look at my mother. What did she ever get out of life. Furthest she ever went was an outing now and again to Locke Park at Barnsley. Do you know, she reckoned it up once, and she said for three years the furthest she ever went was to Titus Healey's shop at the end of our street. What sort of life was that? [*Pause*] Look at Dick's mother. She had to get married when she was eighteen. She was forty-two years old when she had their Clarice. Twenty-four years of married life and she still hadn't done with it. Look at her now. On her deathbed. A life-time of bringing kids up. She's had no life of her own at all. [*Pause*] And talk about bitter. She might be dying but she's still got a tongue like an adder. What a temper. Dick's dad was that late home one dinner-time that she ran up to the Hare and Hounds in her pinny with his plate in her hand and plonked it down on t'table in front of him. [*Pause*] And do you know what he said?

Joe: What?

Freda: Have you put any salt on it?

[**Joe** *laughs*]

When she goes, she'd take him with her if she could.

[**Freda** *mangles the pit clothes*]

Well, I don't want that carry on all my life. I want to go some-where, and do summat with my life.

Joe: The club'll not provide you with a maid, you know, if you come to Derby.

Freda: I know that. I don't want a maid. But things'd be dif-ferent if we could get away from here. [*Pause*] At least I'd be sure he'd be coming home every day, wouldn't I? There's not that many men get killed playing at football. [*Pause*] I'd better put his dinner out, he'll be home any time now.

[**Freda** *ladles hash from the pan on to a plate*]

And he wouldn't be able to go out drinking as much, would he, if he was a footballer? He'd have to train and get fit wouldn't he?

George: Does he smoke?

Freda: [*Pause*] Sometimes.

George: Heavy?

Freda: No. He can't afford it.

George: Fatal. Smoking and drinking for an athlete.

Freda: He might not want to go out all the time then though, mightn't he? He'd be happier in his work. He might want to spend a bit more time at home. That makes sense don't it?

[*Pause. Neither man answers her*]

[*There is a knock at the door.* **Winnie** *enters*]

Winnie: Has our Stanley come back yet, Freda?

Freda: Yes, I've just sent him up to t'Hare and Hounds to see if Dick's in there.

Winnie: I thought he was a long time. [*Pause*] You haven't found him yet then?

Freda: He'll be here in a minute. His dinner's served out ready.

Winnie: I don't know. You want to take a firm hold of him, make him settle down before it's too late. How long have you been married, five months? And. . . .

Freda: Seven. Seven months.

Winnie: Seven months, a bairn on the way and he's at it already. Out at all hours, rolling home singing and shouting. Missing his dinner. Our Walter's been home an hour now.

Freda: I'll send your Stanley round as soon as he gets back then.

Winnie: You've got to be firm with 'em. Let 'em know who's t'boss. They'll have you up a stick if you let 'em. [*Silence in the house*] Is there owt else I can do for you, Freda?

Freda: No. Not just now. I'll send your Stanley in as soon as he comes back.

Winnie: Right, love. If there's owt else you want, just give a knock.

[*She goes out, closing the door behind her.* **Freda** *waits a few seconds before she speaks*]

Freda: Their Walter. He's nowt but a doormat. Anybody'll tell you that.

George: At least she knows where he is.

Freda: She's just jealous that's all. Their Walter. Who'd want to be married to an article like that?

George: Why hasn't your husband ever signed for anybody, Mrs Hayes? [*Pause.* **Freda** *does not answer him*] He can play a bit you know.

Freda: I know that. He knows it an'all. [*Pause*] But he don't take it seriously. He don't take owt seriously.

Joe: I can't understand that when his only choice is the pit.

Freda: I know, but he won't budge from round here. He gets ten shillings a match for Saturday afternoon. He doesn't have to train. He's proud of that, not having to train. He thinks it's clever. He's got his mates. And his beer. [*Pause*] I think he's scared of risking it just in case he fails.

Joe: He can always come back if he don't make it.

Freda: No. [*Pause*] It's easier to think that you could have made it, than to know that you didn't.

Joe: Well, we think he could make it, don't we, George?

[**George** *does not answer him*]

Freda: I wish you'd try and tell him that.

George: That's what we came for, but it looks as though we've backed a loser.

Freda: Oh no. Don't say that. He might listen to you. I mean, it's a long way to come from Derby. It might make him think again.

George: We're not going to have time to make him think owt, unless he comes home in the next few minutes.

Freda: He'll be in anytime now, he's bound to be.

Joe: That kid's taking his time isn't he?

George: He's probably spent that penny and buggered off. I bet he's stood up an entry with his finger stuck into a bag of kali or summat.

Freda: No, he wouldn't do that. He's a good lad. He does as he's told does young Stanley. [*Pause*] Do you want another pot of tea while you're waiting? I'll pop t'kettle on and mash some fresh.

George: No thanks, missus. We haven't got time.

Freda: Well. [*Pause*] I'll just try and get done then, ready for when he comes in. He hates coming. . . .

[*There is a knock at the door*]

Come in, love!

[**Stanley** *opens the door and comes in*]

Did you find him?

Stanley: [*He has to get his breath back before he can speak. Then, panting heavily*] No, he'd been in the Star, but he'd gone.

Freda: Did they know where to?

Stanley: No. They said he'd gone out with Mr Mott.

Freda: I'll give him Mr Mott when he comes in.

Stanley: He'd not been anywhere else though.

Freda: Did you try their house?

Stanley: Who's house?

Freda: Tommy Mott's.

Stanley: No, you didn't ask me to go there.

Freda: He could be there. Or he could be down t'gardens at Tommy's pigeon hut.

George: It sounds as though you're married to the Scarlet Pimpernel to me, missus. He could be here. He could be there. He could be anywhere by the sounds of it. I think it's time we were off.

[*There is a pause while he stands up. Then* **Joe** *stands up*]

Freda: Hey, don't go yet. It'll not take him a minute to run down to Tommy's house, and then to t'gardens.

George: We haven't got time. We'll miss the bus if we stop any longer.

Freda: It'll not take him a minute.

George: The lad'll be worn to a frazzle if he does any more running. Look at him. He's like a skinned rabbit as it is.

Freda: He doesn't mind, do you, love? He's always running errands for me.

George: No. After all, missus, he did know we were coming.

Freda: He's had to swap shifts. I told you that. You can't blame him for that, can you?

George: I'm not blaming him for owt. But I said we'd come Monday dinner-time, and he said he'd be in.

Freda: He's probably got t'wrong day. Perhaps he thinks you're coming another day.

George: I wouldn't think so. It doesn't take much remembering from Saturday to Monday does it?

Freda: Perhaps he's forgot. He's got a lot on his mind you know, what with his mother badly and all that.

George: Well, he don't seem to be worrying too much about her. I notice you haven't sent the lad round to see if he's called in there.

Freda: I can do though. That's where he probably is. It's only in the next street. Stanley. . . . ?

George: No. Don't bother lad. We've no time now.

Joe : Is it still raining, son?

George : Either that, or he's sweating heavy.

Freda: What shall I tell him when he comes in?

George: Tell him that we came to see him like we said we would.

Freda: Can I arrange for him to see you sometime? Perhaps he could come to Sheffield to see you? He's on days next week. He could come one afternoon.

George: We'll let you know.

Freda: Will you come and watch him again?

George: We've no need to watch him anymore. We know enough about him now.

Freda: Will you come back?

George: I don't know. We've a lot of players to see. A lot of reports to follow up. We'll let you know if we want to come up again.

[*He opens the door. It is still raining*]

Joe: Thanks for the tea, missus. [*Pause*] Look at it. We'll get drenched walking to the bus stop.

George: We'll get drenched if we miss it and have to walk to Sheffield Lane Top. Come on.

[*They leave the house*]

Joe: [*From outside*] Ta-ra Mrs Hayes. We might see you again sometime.

[*We hear them walking away down the street in the rain. Then* **Freda** *closes the door*]

Freda: [*Quietly*] Just wait. Just wait till he comes in. [*Pause*] You'd better go home now, Stanley. Your mam'll be wondering where you are.

Stanley: Can I have that other penny now?

Freda: What other penny?

Stanley: That one. He said I could have it if I hurried up.

Freda: Of course you can have it.

Stanley: I went as fast as I could.

Freda: I know you did, love. It wasn't your fault.

[*She opens the door for him*]

Off you go now. And dry your hair when you get in. I don't want you catching your death of cold on my account.

[*She watches him go, then closes the door after him. Pause*]

Just wait till he gets in. I'll kill him. I will. I'll murder him. It's not fair on him. It's just not right. [*Pause while she thinks how to get back on him*] And if he thinks he's having his dinner in this house, he's another think coming.

[*She scrapes the food off the plate on to the fire*]

And he can get washed in cold water.

[*She pours the pan of hot water down the sink*]

Football. I'll give him bloody football. Where's them boots?

[**Freda** *throws back the cupboard doors and scrambles about inside*]

Right.

[*She takes them to the fire and throws them on*]

You'll not play in them again. [*Pause while she watches them*] Go on, burn you buggers, burn.

[*As she stands there watching them she begins to realize the consequences of what she has done*]

Christ, quick.

[*She pulls them off and they clatter into the hearth. Then she picks them up and runs with them to the sink. She runs the tap onto them. She turns the tap off*]

They're not too bad. He'll never notice if I rub a bit of muck on 'em.

[*She puts the boots into the cupboard and closes the doors*]

[*Pause while she considers what to do next. There is nothing else to do, but carry on working*]

Well, this is not going to buy the baby a bonnet, standing here doing nowt.

[*She takes some clothes out of a tub and starts to mangle them. We hear the squeezed water running back into the tub and the mangle turning*]

[*Quietly*] What a life.

The End

Loyalties

Peter McDougall

Characters

Onnie, a 15-year-old Scots boy
Father ⎫
Mother ⎭ Onnie's parents
Wylie, a policeman, who is also a neighbour
Patsie Gallahar, a friend of Onnie's, aged 26
Two Boys, Onnie's age
Barman
Drunk
Young Policeman
Other Drunks

First televised on BBC 1, 23 February 1978

Loyalties

Scene: **The Street.** *The street is in a small grey town built into the hills overlooking the grey sea. The main street of the town runs along the shoreline and is constantly windy, wet with the spray from breakers battering the sea wall and facing (off-shore on the horizon) three looming, demonic, lifelessly grey oil platforms. The street of this first scene is of drab, identical council houses overlooking the sea and the platforms. The houses are reasonably neat – a good respectable sheen on the windows and extravagant window displays hint at pretentions. The street swarms with children. Girls with skirts tucked in their knickers jump over a bounding ball, chanting rhythms of timing. Younger girls teeter about on their mothers' borrowed high heels, head scarves knotted under their chins, handbags dangling from arms, tipping them as they shuffle about in their dream bungalows of a single line of broken and chipped bricks – four for a table, two for a chair, bean tins and rags for the necessary silverware and table-cloths. In house No. 15 we hear the unintelligible near-hysterical raised voices of a man and woman. They suddenly stop and* **Onnie** *comes out of the house. He stands on the step, red-faced and breathing fast with anger. He is a boy of fifteen with the ungainly attributes of adolescence, eyes and mood dull with indecision. He stands for a second, turns abruptly and walks back into the house.*

Scene: **Onnie's house.**   *The* **Mother** *is bent over, prowling in a drawer. The* **Father** *sits stiffly tense in a chair, obviously irritated from his recent exertions. Both of them look up slightly surprised as* **Onnie** *bursts back in through the door shouting*

Onnie: Anyway! how would you know what he's like? . . . Don't even know him!

Father: Back for another round, are ye?

Onnie: You don't know him, though, dae ye?

Mother: Aye better'n you think maybe! . . . You don't need tae try'n get tae know a man like him, his kind make themselves known tae you.

Onnie: He's ma mate!

Mother: Well get yourself mates ages wae yourself . . . .

[*She bends over and starts rummaging in the drawer again*]

. . . That yin's too old fur you.

Onnie: He's only twenty six'n that's naw old.

Father: Naw, jist the two days older'n the Viennese Waltz. . . .

[*He gets to his feet and points a warning finger at his son*]

. . . Alongside your fifteen, it's old! So jist you keep away from him, Onnie, hear? Cut him adrift.

[**Onnie** *screws up his face in frustration. His question is more of a plea*]

Onnie: But what's wrong wae him?

Mother: Everythin! . . . You think mair o'him than you bliddy-well do o'me.

Father: Us!

[*The* **Mother** *slams the drawer shut, straightens up to face* **Onnie***, ignoring the* **Father's** *indignation at being left out*]

Mother: He's trouble'n so will you be'f you hang about wae him.

Onnie: You don't want me to hive any friends that's aus! We get on taegether. He's a ... well, it's ... ach! You widnae understand anyway.

Father: You're right ... I don't understand the attraction Patsie Gallahar is tae you. He's been in trouble wae the Polis you know.

Onnie: For daft wee things'n who hisnae? But just you tell me what's wrong wae him?

Father: Your mother's told you already.

Onnie: Whut!

Father: Everythin! ... So am warnin' you, keep away frae him.

[*The* **Father** *plonks himself back in his chair and grabs a paper. There is a pause. The* **Mother***, recognizing* **Onnie** *hurt, changes her tack*]

Mother: Listen son, it's jist Patsie Gallahar's a funny man that's aw, disnae hive any friends.

Onnie: Disnae need any.

Father: 'N that's what's funny aboot him!

[*There is a pause. The three of them stare at each other.* **Onnie** *leaves, pulling the door hard behind him. The* **Mother** *and* **Father** *look at each other; the* **Father** *shrugs*]

Scene: **The street.** **Onnie** *walks quickly down the path, away from his house, with a natural gracefulness which his betters would interpret as 'cheek'. The door of No. 20 opens and* **Wylie**

*comes out shouting 'Cheerio' over his shoulder. He is a policeman
in his early forties. His face is red-sore from shaving twice a day.
He walks down his path and out of his gate with the long stride
of a confident man. He sees* **Onnie** *ahead of him, quickens his
step and shouts.*

Wylie: Ho! . . . Onnie son! . . . hod-up. . . .

[**Onnie** *turns around. He is struck with embarrassment at the
sight of the smiling uniform coming down on him: he shuffles
from foot to foot, agitated, digs his hands deep into his pockets
and pulls his head into his shoulders, emphasizing his awkward-
ness.* **Wylie** *catches up, the smile stuck to his face*]

Wylie: . . . 'if you're goin' down the town a'll gae ye a walk in.
Onnie: Aye, sure Mr Wylie.

[*Although* **Onnie** *is obviously not pleased, they walk off together.* **Onnie** *tries to shrink into himself, aware of the silence
and of being seen with a policeman*]

Wylie: What're you doin' with yourself tonight, son?
Onnie: Nothin'.

Scene: **The main street.**   **Onnie** *and* **Wylie** *turn into the main
street of town. It is early evening, everything just closed, and the
street deserted. The pubs will be just filling up. Breakers pound
the sea wall.* **Wylie** *looks at* **Onnie** *questioningly.*

Wylie: No seein' your friend Gallahar tonight?

[**Onnie** *looks away quickly, immediately burdened with
imagined guilts*]

Onnie: I only bump into him from time to time.

Wylie: Oh, aye. . . .

[**Onnie's** *embarrassment increases as he sees, further up the street, the door of a pub open and* **Patsie Gallahar** *step out on to the street.* **Gallahar** *has a face that has travelled around: eyes bright and humorous. He walks off in the other direction. Throwing a glance over his shoulder he sees* **Onnie** *and* **Wylie**. *He stops and leans against the wall of the pub, hands behind his back, one leg tucked up under his other. He spits on the pavement and watches* **Onnie** *and* **Wylie** *walk towards him.* **Onnie**, *still with his hands dug deep in his pockets and trying to pretend that* **Wylie** *is not there, now tries to pretend he doesn't see* **Gallahar** *either.* **Wylie** *smiles at him*]

Wylie: . . . There's a timely bump, eh?

[**Onnie** *looks at him defiantly*]

Onnie: A'm his mate, Mr Wylie!

Wylie: Is he yours?

[*As they reach the pub,* **Onnie** *moves from* **Wylie's** *side and edges his way towards* **Gallahar**. **Wylie** *stares at* **Gallahar**; **Gallahar** *smiles back good-humouredly and spits on the pavement.* **Onnie** *watches both of them expectantly*]

Wylie: You heard aboot the oil-men?

Gallahar: They struck oil?

Wylie: 'N the last couple of weeks a couple o'them've been mugged leavin' this pub . . . They're a fierce bunch of men . . . you be careful who you pick on Gallahar. . . .

[**Wylie** *stares at him, waiting for reaction, but* **Gallahar** *only smiles.* **Onnie**, *slightly surprised, is on the verge of protest, but* **Wylie** *speaks first, without taking his eyes off* **Gallahar**]

. . . A'll see you later Onnie son.

[**Wylie** *walks away and, watched by both of them disappears around a corner.* **Onnie** *scowls;* **Gallahar** *still has the same pleasant smile.* **Onnie** *turns and speaks indignantly*]

Onnie: He accused you o' that! Should've said somethin' tae him . . . Rotten big swine!

[**Gallahar** *pushes* **Onnie** *affectionately*]

Gallahar: He's naw a bad man so don't you turn him intae one bi thinkin' bad things aboot him. Where were you goin' anyway?

Onnie: Jist oota' walk.

Gallahar: Where's your mates?

[**Onnie** *flushes slightly and looks embarrassed*]

Onnie: They're stayin' in tonight.

Gallahar: Well . . . a'm naw dain' anythin' for a couple of hours, want tae come with me'n watch the birds.

[**Onnie** *looks about, trying to be casual, but immediately brightens in spite of himself. They smile at each other and walk off*]

Scene: **The pigeon loft.**   *Behind the sea-front houses, back-greens stretch to the shore. Lines of zig-zagging washing hang across the greens. At the bottom of one green and facing out to sea is a tall, two-storied pigeon loft. A few birds are in the air circling their home and two of them are shuffling up and down the stoop of the loft contemplating flight.* **Onnie** *and* **Gallahar** *come through the entry of the building and duck the hanging washing on their way to the loft.* **Gallahar** *stops, bends over, picks up a long clothes-pole, fits the V into the line and pushes the sagging string up into the air.* **Onnie** *jumps onto the sea-wall* *beside the hut.* **Gallahar**, *covering his eyes with his hand, looks to the sky for his birds.*

Onnie: You like them birds don't you?

Gallahar: They're aw-right. But I don't prefer them tae people 're any o'that flannel 'f that's what you're gettin' at.

Onnie: Naw, naw, honest. . . . I didnae mean that. It's just . . . well, what'd'you think it is that people, you know, don't like aboot you very much?

[**Gallahar** *smiles, walks to the side and squints up at the sky from another angle*]

Gallahar: Don't know son. You'd need tae ask them at've been talkin tae you aboot me.

[*He clicks his fingers at the sky and simultaneously makes a cooing noise by blowing into his cheeks, keeping his mouth closed and letting the noise resound in his ballooned cheeks.* **Onnie** *jumps down from the wall, concerned*]

Onnie: Don't get me wrong! A wis only meanin' well. . . . A worry aboot people liking me, even people a don't know! A go aboot hoping they think a'm nice or tough 're look good, know?

[**Gallahar** *stops cooing and smiles sympathetically at* **Onnie**]

Gallahar: Terrible bein' a man, eh?

[*He clicks his fingers a couple of times, whistles sharply, and turns back to* **Onnie**]

Gallahar: . . . Should learn tae like yourself 'n that'll pass, you'll stop puttin' on a show for other people. . . .

[*He continues his clicking and cooing, directed at the same pigeon*]

. . . Anyway, who's been talkin' about me?

Onnie: Ach! . . . well, was ma father but he's an aul twit anyway. Thinks he knows everythin' about everythin'.

Gallahar: He probably does.

Onnie: Well, you don't if you believe that.

[**Gallahar** *laughs, pushes* **Onnie** *aside and moves round for a better view of his bird*]

Gallahar: Well . . . look at this place. If you've been brought up'n lived in a wee town as tiny as this aw your life, then it becomes the biggest place in the world.

[**Onnie** *spits and kicks a stone in disgust*]

Onnie: What's that to do with my aul man?

Gallahar: He believes he's wordly wise'n he is.

Onnie: But he wis talkin' about you!

Gallahar: So we're talkin' aboot him. . . .

[**Gallahar** *points up at the sky with a finger, picking out the largest pigeon.* **Onnie** *follows his finger*]

. . . That's the big Doo'n he never comes in when a call him . . . He runs rogue.

[*He walks inside the loft leaving* **Onnie** *puzzled*]

[*He climbs up into the loft, opens a cage and takes out a white fan-tailed dove. He strokes it with a finger.* **Onnie's** *voice carries into the loft*]

Onnie: A — but, the thing is ye see, ma father was shoutin'n that aboot you'n. . . . Well, you're a friend in ye? . . . Cannie let him say things aboot a friend, cana? I owe it you tae stand by you!

[**Gallahar** *shouts over his shoulder as he continues to stroke the dove*]

Gallahar: If he's talkin' about me he's leavin' others alone! . . . You're just at an age when you're lookin' for things tae fight with your father about. . . . A'm your excuse, that's aw. . . .

[*He walks to the window of the stoop and looks down on* **Onnie**]

. . . . You don't owe me anythin', son.

[**Onnie,** *looking up at the narrow windows where he can only see* **Gallahar's** *face and hands holding the dove, shouts anxiously*]

Onnie: But a friend's a friend in't he? A mean . . . I know you!

Gallahar: You'd dae better gettin tae know yourself, kid, then when aw them friends let you doon, 'n they will, you except it, aye'n even expect it.

Onnie: Aye sure . . . what's it supposed tae mean though?

Gallahar: Nothin's jist, the less you know yourself the mair you rely on other people'n the harder you get hurt. . . . The big Doo up there, the one I cannie control, this bird here's its mate, its friend . . . watch!

[*He sticks the tail of the dove out of the window, shakes it around making his cooing noise. The big pigeon circles round the loft once, glides in and lands on the stoop.* **Gallahar** *grabs it with his free hand and disappears inside the loft. He comes out of the door at the bottom holding the big blue-grey bird, ruffling its neck feathers with a finger*]

. . . Hundreds of times a've captured it this way'n it still trusts its mate, though.

Onnie: What! . . . you sayin' a shouldnae be loyal tae ma friends cos they'll trick me?

Gallahar: Listen, son, people're loyal tae fitbaw teams, the Masons'n budgies. Loyalty's jist something they . . . draw strength from, find an identity in, you find your own'n get your strength from yourself. . . .

[**Onnie** *looks out at the oil platforms, spits on the ground*]

Onnie: 'n will it help me cope wae that pig o'a father o' mine?

Gallahar: Ahh, there's nothin much wrong with your father, it's you. . . .

[**Onnie** *turns round sharply and is about to speak, stops and watches* **Gallahar** *puzzled.* **Gallahar** *places the pigeon's head in his mouth, blows into it three or four times as though he were giving it the kiss of life and then holds it at arm's length to show the enormously swollen chest to* **Onnie**]

Gallahar: . . . That's how you show their plummage tae full advantage, gottie be careful though, can kill them by doin that . . . nice though, eh?

Onnie: Oh aye, great, listen, what'd'you mean it's me!

Gallahar: Well, up'n till you were twelve you thought your father wis a great guy, right? . . . From twelve to the age you are noo you think he's a swine, but when you reach ma age you're gonnie realize your old man wis a great guy'n everythin he's told you over the years is suddenly gonnie make sense . . . 'cept by the time you're ma age and realize it, it's too late.

[**Gallahar** *turns away and walks into the loft with the pigeon. He pulls open a cage and puts the bird in.* **Onnie's** *voice carries in from outside*]

Onnie: That's aw very well fur you but you don't hive tae listen to his daft advice, it gies me brain dammage!

Gallahar: You don't listen tae it anyway!

[*He locks the cage, turns around and stands in the door of the loft, looking out at* **Onnie**. **Onnie** *looks at him shyly*]

Onnie: A'd listen tae any advice you gave me, though.

Gallahar: Wid you now. . . .

[*He steps out and turns his back on* **Onnie** *as he starts to lock up the door of the loft. He speaks over his shoulder*]

Gallahar: . . . Well, you're talkin' a lot aboot friendship 'n aw the rest o'it, but if you want a real friend . . . try your father, cos everybody else is only subs.

[*He straightens up and turns round, smiling at* **Onnie**. **Onnie** *stares at him questioningly*]

Onnie: Ach! A don't un. . . .

[**Gallahar** *pushing* **Onnie** *in front of him, starts walking away from the hut*]

Gallahar: Why's a sub a sub?

Onnie: Cos he cannie make the first team.

Gallahar: That's it. . . .

[*He puts his hand on* **Onnie's** *shoulder and bends him over as they pass under a whipping sheet on a clothes-line*]

. . . A'm off tae the boozer. Where are you goin' yourself?

Onnie: Well a'm jist, you know, walk aboot a bit.

Gallahar: O.K. A'll away this way. See you later kid, eh?. . . .

[*He turns and walks away, stops, then turns back*]

. . . Hive you any money?

[**Onnie**, *thinking he's being tapped, immediately flushes. He slaps his hands against both pockets, near panicking*]

Onnie: Naw, naw honest, I just. . . .

[**Gallahar** *walks back towards him, goes through his pockets and takes out a quid. He sticks it into* **Onnie's** *top pocket*]

. . . it's awright I don't!. . . .

Gallahar: Go tae a café or somethin'. A'll see you later, eh?

[*There is a pause.* **Gallahar** *smiles at* **Onnie's** *troubled face*]

. . . Don't look so troubled kid . . . you're carryin the weight o' your age that's aw, but don't worry about it cos as you get older . . . it just gets heavier.

[*He walks off laughing aloud at his joke, ducking beneath the hanging washing.* **Onnie** *watches after him, then turns, walks back to the loft and vaults over the sea wall out of view*]

Scene: **The Seafront, early evening.**   **Onnie** *has tied four pieces of string onto the corners of a rumpled hanky. As he walks along the beach he searches the ground until he finds a smooth stone: he picks it up and ties it to the ends of the string. He continues to walk, grabs the hanky in its centre, swings it round a couple of times in a full arc and mouths an audible 'swish' as the parachute leaves his hand and soars into the air. He smiles as it opens out and floats effortlessly to the ground. He picks it up and starts to swing it again as he continues to walk. It is dusk.* **Onnie** *comes to the pub and stands outside. He looks at the warm smoky glow of light shining out from the pub window into the near-darkened street. Each time someone leaves or enters, the rumbling noise from the Friday-night-out crowds bursts out into the quiet of the* *street.* **Onnie** *strains each time the door opens, trying to catch a glimpse inside. In the end he walks on, hands dug deep in his pockets. By now it is night.* **Onnie** *walks along the street, hands still in his pockets. He looks up and sees ahead* **Two Boys** *of his own age leaning against the brightly lit window of the café.* **Onnie** *immediately straightens up, takes his hands out of his pockets and walks towards them with a deliberate stagger. The* **Two Boys** *push themselves up off the window as* **Onnie** *swaggers towards them.*

First Boy: Hiya Onnie! . . . Where've you been aw these days?

Second Boy: Aye, naw seen you fur ages.

[**Onnie** *takes up a hard-man stance in front of them and shrugs casually*]

Onnie: A've been around, oot wae ma mate Patsie, know? Patsie Gallahar.

[*Both* **Boys** *looked slightly surprised and envious*]

First Boy: God, you runnin' aboot wae him?

Second Boy: He's a bit o' a hard case int he? What's he like, eh?

First Boy: Bet you feel pretty good knockin' aboot wae him.

Onnie: Ach, it's naw that, we work the pigeons together, know?

First Boy: He's a good man tae keep away frae int he?

[**Onnie** *smiles patronizingly and spits on the pavement*]

Onnie: Ah . . . he's aw right when you know him as well as a dae. . . . See youse!

[*He swaggers into the cafe, leaving the* **Boys** *looking after him admiringly*]

Scene: | **Outside the pub.** | *The double doors of the pub are pinned back, a bell is ringing inside, drunks are hanging on to each other outside making tomorrow's arrangements for further drinking meetings. The odd voice is raised in song. The* **Barman's** *voice screams over all the other sounds.*

Barman: Right, you men! . . . Clear the place! . . . Back to your corrals!

[*Men continue to shout and pour out of the doors. Farewells are shouted in the street.* **Gallahar** *comes out of the pub. He is conspicuous because of his ability to walk straight. He walks to the end of the building and disappears down an entry. The doors of the pub are closed.* **Onnie** *having left the café, approaches the pub along the street. One of the doors opens, casting a square of light onto the black pavement, and the last* **Drunk** *sways out in front of* **Onnie.** *A big man in jeans and work-jacket, he walks off down the road, swinging, and turns into the entry. Without noticing that he is doing so,* **Onnie** *follows him – still with his head hung and wrapped in his thoughts. The* **Drunk** *reaches the bottom of the entry and turns right into the sea-front car park.* **Onnie** *reaches the mouth of the entry, looks up and stops, surprised.* **Gallahar** *has come between him and the* **Drunk.** **Onnie** *watches, puzzled, as* **Gallahar** *at first follows, then starts to run towards the* **Drunk.** *His eyes suddenly widen with realization and fright. He opens his mouth as if to shout. The* **Drunk** *hears the footsteps behind him and, face hanging slack with drink, mumbling and oblivious, he turns. His eyes widen, his mouth falls open and his arms come up to shield his face as he staggers back a couple of steps.* **Onnie** *throws himself back, flat against the wall, snaps his head away to the side, grimacing, his face screwed up. He shakes his head clear, then peers around the corner. The* **Drunk** *is sprawled on the ground;* **Gallahar** *is bent over him going through a pocket.* **Onnie** *turns and runs back up the entry, around the corner and back into the street. As he* *runs past the pub and along the length of the street,* **Onnie** *is watched through the windshield of a car. A radio-phone crackles in the car, an arm reaches over, switches it off and throws open the car door.* **Wylie** *gets out of the Panda Car, crosses the road and disappears down the entry.* **Onnie** *continues on up his own street towards his house. Suddenly he stops and steps in beside a hedge. His breathing becomes fast and the noise of his heart is loud in his ears. The Panda Car lies outside No. 15*]

Scene: **Onnie's house.** **Onnie's Father** *and* **Wylie** *sit across from each other both looking into the fire. The door opens and the* **Mother** *comes in with a tray of tea. She lays it down on the table, takes a biscuit, dunks it in one of the cups and throws it into her face. The* **Father** *leans over, lifts off his tea, tastes some and grimaces.*

Father: But that means he saw it! An' he's hardly gonnie be a witness against his hero is he?

Wylie: The way Onnie came runnin' oota that entry he'd obviously got a fright.

Father: 's naw a fright he needs, it's a shock. . . . . So what'll happen to Gallahar?

Wylie: Nothin' much. He'll get fined for brawling, a mean, the guy wis that drunk he cannie remember anythin' about it, he's only got a black eye'n a lack of money, and he's naw even sure if he had any money or if he spent it. So Gallahar'll say that they were in the pub together, the guy started insulting his pigeons'n they went out to the car park to do battle.

Father: But you said the fella was definitely rolled.

Wylie: He was . . . 'n I don't want this to sound bad, John, but, some o' these oil men, well . . . in a lot o' ways they ask fur it, they're flash, aie drunk'n a hella'va nuisance, there's a couple o'them a widnae mind tannin' maself.

[*The **Father** gets up from his chair and paces erratically*]

Father: Aye, aye, Tam. OK, so they're all cowboys, am no concerned wae them . . . so if Onnie saw Gallahar doin' it?

Wylie: If he did then . . . well, whether you like it or no, John, Onnie'n Gallahar are mates'n Onnie's young, it'd hurt him a lot . . . you'd be gettin him to turn against his friend.

Mother: An' he'd never dae that wid he? Oh naw, he'd turn against me quick. . . .

Father: Us!

Mother: . . . enough, but never 'his friend'.

[*There is a pause; the **Father** stops his pacing long enough to look at **Wylie***]

Father: Listen, Tam, a'd rather Onnie be hurt now when he can get over it than hurt himself permanently, which is on the cards if he keeps in wae that Patsie Gallahar. . . .

[*Again he looks at **Wylie** appealingly*]

. . . You know your stuff Tam, you'd be doin' me a favour.

Mother: Us!

[*The **Mother** and **Father** look at **Wylie** expectantly*]

Scene: **The sea front.   Onnie** *is hanging over the sea front hand-rail. The pound note bobs around effortlessly beneath him in the water. He periodically aims and drops spit on it. He is suddenly illuminated by a beam of light: he turns round, shielding his eyes with a hand. The torch-beam is turned off and* **Onnie** *sees* **Wylie** *standing beside the open door of the Panda Car, smiling.*

Wylie: OK, Onnie, son, in you come. . . .

[*Without any sign of protest,* **Onnie** *walks to the car.* **Wylie** *stands aside to let him in*]

. . . Nice night, eh?

Scene: **An inner room at the police station.** **Onnie** *sits alone in a square, stark characterless little room. There is a table and two chairs. The door opens and* **Wylie** *comes in with two mugs of tea. He sets them on the table, then sits opposite* **Onnie.**

Wylie: Drink up, son, there's plenty of sugar in it, mair'n a can say for your mother's tea.

[**Onnie** *looks up at him questioningly over the top of his cup*]

. . . I was just up to see her . . . and your father.

Onnie: What did you want to see them aboot?

Wylie: You know, 'bout that guy that wis beaten up in the car park.

[**Onnie** *flushes slightly but tries to look suitably surprised*]

Onnie: When did that. . . .

[**Wylie** *smiles sympathetically and waves a hand*]

Wylie: Listen son, we've been neighbours for a long time'n you're a good boy, if it was somebody else I might let them talk themselves intae trouble but tae save you embarrassment let me tell you . . . I saw you runnin' oot the entry, I know you saw the mugging . . . or wis it just a fight?

Onnie: It was dark, Mr Wylie. I just saw a couple of guys and heard shouts so I legged it out o' there.

[*There is a pause.* **Onnie** *hesitates, unsure*]

Wylie: It was Gallahar.

Onnie: Naw it wisnae honest, I would've known him widn't a? We're mates a mean, it was two guys aw right but he wasn't one of them.

Wylie: Funny that isn't it? . . . A mean, you his mate cannie even recognize him . . . aye funny, cos he recognized you.

[**Onnie** *looks up, startled and confused*]

Onnie: What'd you mean! You been talkin' tae him?

Wylie: Talkin' tae him! I caught him, he's in a room next door, says he was walking through the car park and found the drunk man lying there, sais he saw you standing in the entry so you had seen him find the drunk . . . . But you didn't recognize him, right?

[**Onnie** *looks about him, slightly flustered*]

Onnie: I didn't mean, I don't know how a can be sure, it might've been him and. . . .

Wylie: But you said you only heard shouts, so if Gallahar did find the man what was he shouting for, an ambulance? You're trying to protect him, son, it's silly.

[**Onnie** *is now on the verge of panicking*]

Onnie: A'm naw, really am naw, just tryin' tae think what happened.

[**Wylie** *makes a show of shaking his head, getting laboriously to his feet and pacing about with his hands clasped behind his back*]

Wylie: A know he's your friend son, but that's no reason to get yourself intae trouble. He's next door, caught! You say you don't know what happened cos it wis dark. But he says you can verify the fact that he stumbled across the man accidentally. It's down to you, son . . . if you didn't recognize him, you didn't, but he recognized you. What's it to be?

[**Onnie** *has a tortured expression on his face, obviously torn*]

Onnie: A . . . a . . . didnae see who it wis – a mean, he might've. . . .

Wylie: You didn't recognize him! . . .

[**Wylie** *stands above* **Onnie**, *looking down at him.* **Onnie** *melts under the stare and nods a 'yes'*]

. . . Right! A'll go'on question Gallahar again, tell him he hasnae a witness.

[**Wylie** *walks out of the room.* **Onnie** *wrings his hands with dread*]

Scene: **The front desk at the police station.**   **Wylie** *walks down the corridor and leans in at the front desk. A* **Young Policeman** *is doing paperwork.*

Wylie: Listen, go'n find Gallahar'n bring him in.

[**Wylie** *turns back the way he came and walks off*]

Scene: **An inner room in the police station.**

Wylie: Well . . . at first he was angry and just kept calling you a liar but, without you to back him up he was just shoutin' in the dark. . . .

[*For the first time he looks up at* **Onnie**, *smiles*]

. . . Aw these tough guys are only tough'n their home grounds anyway, he mugged the man all right, saw you'n the entry thought you'd back him up. . . . When you tell lies Onnie, even although it was to protect him, it's only a matter of time before you trip yourself up . . . let's have it this time, the truth. . . . Always tell the truth Onnie!

[**Onnie***'s head is hung. He speaks into the table*]

Onnie: A wis walkin' hame, the drunk was up ahead of me, when a got into the car park somehow Patsie had got between me'n the drunk. . . . he must've been waiting for him. . . .

[*He looks up at* **Wylie** *but* **Wylie** *is impassive*]

Scene: **Outside the police station.**   **Onnie** *walks down the steps of the police station and across the street. A Panda Car comes from the opposite direction and pulls up outside the station.* **Onnie** *looks back over his shoulder. He stops and sees the* **Young Policeman** *get out of the car, walk round to the other side and open the door.* **Gallahar** *gets out.* **Onnie** *looks on, confused, as* **Gallahar** *and the* **Young Policeman** *climb the steps of the station.*

Scene: **The pigeon loft.**   *It is daytime. The day is grey and overcast; the sea is choppy.* **Gallahar** *stands outside his loft cooing at the sky and flying his birds. In between he whistles to himself.* **Onnie** *stands outside the pigeon enclosure watching* **Gallahar***. When* **Gallahar** *turns suddenly following the flight of a bird,* **Onnie** *ducks out of sight.* **Gallahar** *is unaware of his presence. Eventually* **Onnie** *emerges;* **Gallahar** *stares at the frightened boy as* **Onnie***'s words pour uncontrollably.*

Onnie: You can punch me if you like, but jist didnae know you were in the other room.

[Gallahar *walks quickly towards him, waving a hand for quiet*]

Gallahar: Hey, hey, hey. . . . Come on, kid, what you on aboot? Eh?

Onnie: Aw that carry-on with the polis, wisnae ma fault, they told me. . . .

[Gallahar *slaps* Onnie *on the shoulder*]

Gallahar: Hey, behave yourself . . . they pulled an old trick on you, that's aw. I wouldn't hold that against you, Jesus. . . . Calm down, now.

[*He smiles and turns to look up at the sky*]

Onnie: I feel bad about it, that's aw. I think they're swines for tricking me like that, a mean, if the positions 'ave been reversed, you widnae've been tricked'n you would've backed me up, widn't you?

Gallahar: Forget it, Onnie.

[*He turns away and walks inside the loft.* Onnie *follows eagerly and stands in the doorway, face anxious, watching* Gallahar. Gallahar *has his back to* Onnie *and is bending over one of the cages.* Onnie *shouts at his back*]

Onnie: But you wid've lied for me wouldn't you?

[Gallahar *straightens up, holding the big pigeon in his hands. He looks at* Onnie *questioningly, then shakes his head slightly*]

Gallahar: You jist wint leave it alone will you kid.

[*He walks past* Onnie *out of the loft.* Onnie *turns and immediately follows. A note of desperation creeps into his voice*]

Onnie: But how can I. They tricked me intae gettin' you fur them.

[**Gallahar** *throws his arms in the air releasing the big pigeon. It makes off with a noisy flutter.* **Gallahar** *watches after it smiling. He then jumps up into a sitting position on the sea-wall and looks down at* **Onnie,** *smiling*]

Gallahar: Listen, Onnie, don't get upset about the polis cos. . . .

Onnie: Ach! You're always sayin' not to get upset, gettin' tae sound like ma father.

Gallahar: . . . Cos it's you! . . . not the polis, 'n that's why
, you're carryin' on like this, it's guilt.

Onnie: What?

Gallahar: It's you, kid . . . you're the one who goes on about trustin' friendships and by the demands you put on it you let me down. I don't think so, mind, but you do. The police didn't trick you.

Onnie: But Wylie told me he had you in the other room and he didn't.

Gallahar: But that didn't matter cos you didn't know. By telling you what he did, he fixed up a set of circumstances that wid test your loyalty tae me, he asked you very simply if you saw me belt the guy or come across him accidently, if you said you saw me belt him, fine! If you said I found the bloke lyin' there, great! It widnae've made any difference tae me, mind, but you widnae be feelin' the way you are now cos in your own eyes, you would've been loyal tae me.

Onnie: A – but! It wisnae as simple as that!

[**Gallahar** *grins, jumps down from the wall and looks back up at the sky*]

Gallahar: A – but it wis son'n whut's gettin up your nose is that you took tne easy way oot, you lied for yourself, to save yourself embarrassment and trouble and that's fine tae, so stop eatin' at yourself.

[*He starts to walk about, his eyes on the sky, clicking his fingers and making his cooing noise. There is a pause.* **Onnie**, *eyes on the ground, kicks a stone in frustration*]

Onnie: Would you've lied for me?

Gallahar: You're no me'n you wouldn'tve been in that position.

Onnie: But would you've though?

Gallahar: Aye! . . . A wid've lied, but not for you! A wid've lied, just to screw up the polis cos it'd be the natural thing for me to do . . . anyway. . . . Wylie knew it was me'n could've picked me up anytime. . . . He probably set the whole thing up for your benefit so's you wouldn't hang around me anymore.

[*There is a pause.* **Gallahar** *still looks up at the sky*]

Onnie: Well . . . he didn't need to go to all that trouble. When I saw you punch that man, that was enough. . . . Just thought you were different.

[**Gallahar**, *still with his eyes on the sky and cooing a couple of times, speaks to* **Onnie** *without taking his eyes away from the sky*]

Gallahar: The rogue pigeon up there, he's been wild for so long he's predictable . . . . 's become ordinary. See you kid.

[**Onnie** *stands for a second; he then turns and walks off through the back-greens, followed by the noise of* **Gallahar's** *clicking fingers and cooing noise*]

Scene: **The street.**   **Onnie** *walks dejectedly along the sea front towards the café. The* **Two Boys** *come out and walk quickly away in the opposite direction.* **Onnie** *immediately brightens and shouts to them.*

Onnie: Ho! . . .

[*They stop and turn around*]

Onnie: . . . Where's youse off to!?

First Boy: There's a band playin' in the Toon-Hall the night, goin' tae get tickets.

Second Boy: Fancy it?

Onnie: Aye!

First Boy: Mon then!

[*They turn away and continue walking.* **Onnie** *pulls his hands out of his pockets and runs to catch up*]

The End

Family Ties (a double bill)
Wrong First Time

Peter Terson

Characters

Frank Larson, referred to as Dad
Mrs Larson, referred to as Mum
Emily
Sandra } their married daughters
Penny, their youngest daughter
Claude, Emily's husband
Smudge, Sandra's husband
Barry, Penny's boyfriend
Mr Bellamy, Barry's father, referred to as Father
Mrs Bellamy, Barry's mother, referred to as Mother

First performed by the National Youth Theatre at the
Round House Downstairs, 18 August 1977

Wrong First Time

Scene: **The Larsons' house.** **Dad** – *Frank Larson – is in the sitting room with* **Mum**.

Dad: I have a theory to postulate. In fact it's more than a theory, it's a dead certainty. Culled from observation and experience my theory is this. . . . 'Girls always marry the wrong man first time round.'

Mum: What you on about?

Dad: My new social theory – girls *always* marry the wrong man first time round.

Mum: Nonsense.

Dad: What answer is that? Give me facts to contradict my argument. Give me statistics.

Mum: You see lovely couples together every day of the week, boys and girls, holding hands, cuddling in the park.

Dad: Cuddling in the park is not marriage. I'm not talking about *love*, I'm talking about *marriage*. The Solemn Oath. Oh, girls often fall in love with the right boy first time round but they inevitably progress to marry the wrong bloke.

Mum: What about you and me? We've lasted.

Dad: Yeah, but this proves my point. I'm your *second husband*.

Mum: I was happy with my first husband until he drowned at Torquay.

Dad: It was wearing thin, though, before the sea claimed him. Be honest.

Mum: I was seeing through him a bit, yes.

Dad: And you'd only been married six months.

Mum: Seven nearly. Strange, him drowning like that when he was a swimming instructor himself. Providence I call it.

Dad: It wasn't providence, it was swimming with a bellyful of beer and chips.

Mum: He did all the wrong things that day. Went into an icy sea after lunch with the Red warning flag up. He didn't get beyond the first line of surf before the cramp hit him.

Dad: Well, there of course, women marry such fools first time round and never see through them until it's too late.

Mum: He looked beautiful in his bathing trunks, though. Muscles like velvet-covered steel.

Dad: That brings me to the second part of my theory. Women marry the wrong bloke first time round because at that age they are so *impressionable.* They fall for blokes for all sorts of silly, impressionable reasons; they fall for blokes because they're specially tall, or specially short, because they're black or have a prison record; because they're weight-lifters, or pop singers or footballers.

Mum: Not *all* girls marry the wrong man first time round, surely.

Dad: All girls.

Mum: What about the Queen? Her marriage has lasted.

Dad: Now that strengthens my argument. . . . Hers was a marriage of *state.* It was arranged and discussed by her elders and advisors. It was approved at Cabinet level. Thus it has stood the test of time. Which brings me to the specific point of my theory — girls are just emotionally unfit to choose their own husbands. They inevitably choose wrong the first time round.

Mum: Fancy *you* saying that . . . the father of two married daughters.

Dad: Well, really, *look* at them. Take our Emily and her choice for life, Claude.

Mum: Claude's a very handsome man.

Dad: Handsome! Oh he's beautiful. Like a statue. And as much intelligence. God gave him a lovely body but forgot to put anything in the head. She can't live with a handsome dummy all her life. I remember the first time she brought him back here, we spent two hours trying to carry on a conversation before we realized he didn't have a thought in his head. We went through a bundle of topics and all he went through was his fingernails with his manicure set. And when we played Scrabble he bit the dust at the first four-letter word. Spent the rest of the night in thoughtless silence combing his hair.

Mum: He likes to look after his appearance.

Dad: Look after his appearance? He had nothing else to look after. I had to remove all the mirrors in the house before he had an accident tripping over himself.

Mum: I'm sure they can be very happy.

Dad: No woman can be happy just *looking* at a husband all her life. One day she'll see through him. The truth will dawn. She'll look straight through his handsome features into his empty head. And she'll think, 'I'm married to a handsome dummy.'

Mum: She's devoted to him.

Dad: Oh, yes. The blindness has been known to last a long time in these marriage cases; but when the veil lifts they throw up their hands in horror. Look at our Sandra and her damned Smudge. What right has any girl got marrying a bloke called Smudge?

Mum: I'll admit he's a little immature.

Dad: Immature! He's the oldest Hell's Angel on the road. She just fell for his speedie image. She'd have been better off marrying the motorbike.

Mum: He'll grow up.

Dad: When? For his last wedding anniversary present he bought himself a new 750 Yamaha motorbike. Call that growing up? He'll not grow up till his chains and medals rust, and they're stainless steel.

Mum: It takes time to make a family man out of a Hell's Angel.

Dad: It didn't take him long to make a family woman out of our Sandra. He gives her a pram and a kid while he has a new model virgin on his pillion.

Mum: You don't give your daughters much hope.

Dad: It's just a matter of seeing which one of them sees the light first.

[*Enter* **Emily** *and* **Claude**. *He is indeed beautiful*]

Emily: Hello, Mum.

Mum: Hello, Emily. Hello, Claude.

[**Claude** *inclines his head*]

Dad: You're back early.

Emily: Claude is fed up.

Dad: Why is Claude fed up?

Emily: He isn't appreciated.

Mum: You appreciate him.

Emily: But the General Public doesn't appreciate him.

Dad: He can't make a living out of being appreciated.

Emily: The world isn't taking advantage of his appearance and presentation.

Dad: He's certainly tried to make the world notice his presence and presentation. He's applied for every job where he'd be looked at, from film star to sandwich-board man.

Emily: This is the point, he's beginning to think he's wasted himself on the masses.

Dad: I'm one of the masses, he isn't wasted on me.

Mum: Isn't he happy working in the department store any more?

Emily: It's getting on his nerves, selling clothes to men who can't expect to look half as good as he would in them.

Dad: He could apply for a transfer to Ladies' Underwear.

Emily: That's a point, Claude, you could ask for a transfer to the Ladies' Department. [*Pause*] No, he isn't keen.

Mum: What are you going to do then?

Emily: We've decided to apply for jobs where appearance counts.

Dad: Bus conductor.

Emily: The coins would soil his hands.

Dad: Doorman.

Emily: He'd be trampled on.

Dad: Lift attendant.

Emily: Up and down all day.

Dad: Try putting him in Madame Tussaud's.

Emily: Not funny Dad.

Mum: You have tried an awful lot of jobs where appearance counted but they needed other things.

Dad: Like common sense.

Emily: I think we should try harder to *sell* him.

Dad: That's the best idea yet.

Emily: I mean sell his assets — his good looks, dress sense, style.

Dad: You could sell his personality to Oxfam.

Emily: I'm going to apply for all sorts of jobs for him. . . . I'm having proper notepaper with a letterhead printed at the top. . . .

Dad: Letterhead!

Emily: To make an impression.

Dad: It's what you write in the blank space that makes the impression, not the letterhead.

Emily: I don't think you understand Dad . . . come on, Claude, let's get changed.

Dad: Are you using the bathroom?

Emily: Yes.

Dad: We'll send you up packed lunches. . . .

[*They go*]

Mum: There's no need to employ sarcasm. She's trying her best for him.

Dad: But her best is too good for him. . . . She's wasting the best years of her life on him.

Mum: She's grooming him.

Dad: He's not a show jumper . . . he's got to *work*, not just look good. One day she'll meet a bloke with a few grains of intelligence and she'll fall in love with his mind.

Mum: Do you think it's inevitable? This theory of yours? That they marry the wrong man, then have their eyes opened?

Dad: It is my thesis that a girl goes through a period of blindness like a new-born puppy; it afflicts her when she is choosing her first husband. Sooner or later the film clears; if it's sooner she clears off, if it's later she makes the best of a bad job. . . . Here's the next demonstration and proof roaring up now. . . .

[*There is the sound of a motor-bike*]

Dad: Well, that's my second son-in-law arrived . . . my second daughter will be following on foot with the pram. Now what did she see in that one? A tattooed ape in Nazi regalia. She was blinded by the Iron Crosses. Those studs and chains weigh him down, he buckles at the knees and dare not go near a magnet. When he undresses for bed at night he needs a tin opener.

Mum: He's intelligent enough, though, Frank.

Dad: Oh, he's intelligent enough, but it's all in the wrong direction. He's got a brain in the wrong channels. He understands the mind of a Yamaha 750; he has a phenomenal memory for the burn-up roads of Britain; he can handle facts of the spare parts manual, but as an all round man he's stunted. He's retarded. Here he comes up the garden path dressed like a Panzer storm-trooper; what would you feel if he came up dressed like a Red Indian?

[*Enter* **Smudge** *in full regalia, with tattooed chest and arms*]

Smudge: Hiya, in-laws, thought I might find you at home . . . again. . . . Can I leave your daughter and grandchild with you for a couple of hours?

Mum: Of course you can, Smudge.

Dad: Going on nightshift at the tattooist's, are you?

Smudge: Just having a run with the pack.

Dad: Which pack is that? Cub packs?

Smudge: It's the card pack . . . aces high.

Dad: Who's the joker?

Smudge: Do you know, Dad-in-law, you're abusing your privileged position talking to me like that.

Dad: I like taking risks, my grandfather was an animal trainer.

[*Enter* **Sandra** *with the baby. She was probably once pretty but is now a washed out creature*]

Sandra: Mum, can I put baby upstairs while's he's still asleep?

Mum: Put him in my room, Sandra.

Dad: It'll stink of petrol for a week.

Smudge: I'll be off then, San.

Dad: Must you call her San? It sounds . . . medical.

Smudge: Sandra, I'll be off.

Sandra: See you when I do. Have a good spin.

Smudge: It'll be pretty good, the roads have a fast surface.

Dad: Careful when you go through the sound barrier.

Smudge: You should be proud to be related to me.

Dad: I would have been prouder to be related to the man who first won those medals. . . .

[Smudge *goes*]

Sandra: You shouldn't rile him, Dad. It's his world.

Dad: I'd prefer to see him in a family saloon with you and baby than burning up the road with some fresh fanny on his pillion.

Sandra: I wish you wouldn't say that Dad . . . he's *my* man.

[*She goes*]

Dad: Surely *she* can't stay blind much longer?

Mum: It's not up to *you* to open her eyes.

Dad: Oh no, impossible, impossible. It's a feature of my theory that as they marry blind no amount of talking can convince them. The more you try to persuade them the more blind they become. They must discover their own sight for themselves. In my opinion our two daughters are still gazing in the dark. Our Penny is our last hope . . . she has intelligence, good sense, perception . . . she just *might* marry with her eyes open.

Mum: Not according to *your* theory she won't.

Dad: The exception to prove the rule.

[*Enter* Sandra]

Sandra: Baby's still asleep.

Mum: I could have looked after baby and you could have driven off with Smudge;

Sandra: Oh, I think he had other plans tonight . . . to be with the boys.

Mum: Have you been crying?

Sandra: No, my eyes always water in the wind . . . .

Dad: Has he been misusing you? Cos if he has I'll hammer tin tacks into his tyres.

Sandra: He hasn't been misusing me Dad.

Mum: Anyway, let her fight her own battles, I did.

Dad: You weren't married to a world war relic.

[*Enter* Emily]

Emily: Mum, Sandra. I'm trying Claude in his new interview suit . . . he looks so debonair . . . would you like to see him?

Mum: Oh, I'd love to.

Sandra: I didn't realize he was dressing up.

Emily: Dad, he looks very flashy, would you like to see him?

Dad: No thanks, I haven't got my welder's goggles.

[*They go*]

Dad: So far then, it is a certain fact that girls marry the wrong man first time round; no matter how grotesque he is to the rest of the world he is the perfect specimen of mankind in their eyes; in conclusion . . . there is *no remedy* but let them discover the truth for themselves.

[**Penny**, *the third daughter – fresh, young, hopeful – enters the garden*]

Penny: Dad. . . .

Dad: Penny. . . . Had a good day, love?

Penny: Smashing, Dad.

Dad: Been playing your violin I see.

Penny: It was orchestra practice today, Dad.

Dad: I'm glad one of the family is musical. You've been playing tennis too?

Penny: Yes, it was the school tournament. . . .

Dad: Win? Says he hopefully.

Penny: I got through to the next round.

Dad: And what's in the bag?

Penny: Books, and homework.

Dad: You'll be needing a pack horse to bring your bag home soon.

Penny: Dad, is Mum busy?

Dad: She's looking at the new-style Claude emerging from his chrysallis, why?

Penny: I want to tell you something.

Dad: Oh, what is it?

Penny: I have a boyfriend.

Dad: When do we get to see him?

Penny: Now if you like . . . he's outside.

Dad: Bring him up, you can't have lads hanging outside garden gates, they get bad habits like dogs.

Penny: I'll fetch him . . . his name's Barry . . . I'll bring him . . . be nice to him.

Dad: Does he need special treatment?

Penny: No, but just be nice.

Dad: I'm nice to everybody. . . .

[*She goes*]

Dear God of Fathers with Daughters . . . when she appears with him please make him normal . . . let my little girl have seen him with a clear vision . . . let him not be a rose-coloured spectacled mistake. . . .

[*Enter* **Penny** *with the perfect* **Barry**, *a normal boy*]

Penny: Dad, this is Barry. . . .

Dad: Barry is it? Welcome to the Garden of Peace, Barry.

Barry: Why do you call it the Garden of Peace?

Dad: Because, my boy, I live in a house of women and this is my sanctuary.

Barry: I like it.

Penny: Rather over-embellished though.

Dad: Over-embellished. Are you ashamed of your father? This garden is a work of art.

Barry: It looks a work of art, Mr Larson.

Dad: I am a magpie, my dear boy. Wherever I go in the grey world outside I look for little gems of life to add to my work of art. I pick them up and scurry back to my nest.

Barry: The result blends well.

Dad: It's amazing what you can make out of the waste and disposed refuse of this world if you have the eye of the artist.

Barry: You're a bit of a philosopher.

Dad: I am a student of life; and what are you studying Barry?

Barry: I want to be an architect.

Dad: Do you *want* to be an architect or do you *mean* to be an architect?

Barry: I shall be an architect.

Dad: Good for you. Just remember this one thing, when you're an architect and touring your building sites, *nothing* need ever be wasted. Your offcuts might be material to another man; your waste might be the very wealth to someone else. One man's waste is another man's wants. . . .

Barry: I'll remember, and try to plan by it. . . .

Dad: [*To audience*] Well I'll be blowed. Hope at last. My other two daughters brought home fellers who haven't enough in them to open a bag of nuts, yet I can hold a conversation with this lad. . . . Make yourself at home in my walled domain Barry.

[*He goes*]

Penny: I'm sorry if Dad's embarrassing.

Barry: Embarrassing? No, he's a natural.

Penny: Do you think so? I worry he's a bit of a laugh.

Barry: When you bring boys home?

Penny: No, you're the first boy I've brought home. . . .

Barry: Am I really?

Penny: Yes, and I worried that Dad would be embarrassing. I love him but he talks so different from other dads.

Barry: He talks wiser than other dads.

Penny: And the way he picks things up. Wherever he goes for a walk he sees bits of things — perspex, tin, wood, bricks and stones — and brings them back to decorate the garden.

Barry: It's a fresh approach.

Penny: That statue by the mock well is carved in polystyrene.

Barry: That is the eye of the artist.

Penny: Do you like all this? All the clutter?

Barry: I do like it, because it's real and has personality. My parents' home is bought, fitted, and fixed; not a personal touch to it. But this place has your dad's magic individuality.

Penny: Do you know what the greenhouse is made of?

Barry: I don't know, but it looks like a shrine.

Penny: They were demolishing a church so he got hold of the old windows . . . there's a pew inside.

Barry: God should favour that with a bit of sunshine.

[*They go to it*]

Barry: What does he grow?

Penny: Assorted exotica. Nothing mundane for Dad. Wherever he goes he takes a pair of secateurs in his back pocket and takes cuttings; he has Privet à la Jubilee Park; Kew Garden Shrub; Blenheim House Rose. . . .

Barry: He's such a unique character your dad is . . . is your Mum his true partner in life do you think?

Penny: She thinks he's a bit of a character but she's with him.

Barry: I'd like to grow old like this . . . to be surrounded by things that are a projection of my own personality.

Penny: You shouldn't be thinking of growing old.

Barry: I feel I'm growing older every day, in a nice way, I'd like to think about being happy in my old age with the partner of my life.

Penny: You know what Dad says about marriage, 'You're only happy by accident, miserable by design.'

Barry: Let's not design anything then.

[*They kiss*]

Scene: **A couple of months later.**   **Dad** *and* **Mum** *are talking to each other.*

Dad: I'll say this, as regards my theory . . . if it was five years from now I'd say that Penny and Barry have a chance of making a marriage work first time.

Mum: That's very generous of you.

Dad: Just once let Barry get his training behind him and qualify as an architect and I'd say she could have broken the rule and married the right man first time round.

Mum: You sound like the patron saint of wedlock, you do.

Dad: My first two daughters aren't a good advertisement . . . one of them is the matron to a motor-cycle pack and the other is trying to find employment for a tailor's dummy. Penny is our hope. Perhaps with the first one *we* made the mistake in bringing her up. The second one made her own mistakes. The third has learnt from the other two and could well be perfect.

[**Penny** *enters cautiously, thoughtfully*]

Penny: Hello Mum, Dad.

Dad: Hello, love, another day whisked by?

Penny: It dragged a bit Dad.

Dad: Wait till you get to our age, it flies past.

Mum: Everything goes quicker at our age.

Dad: That's true, brain cells; wind; faculties; control. Everything goes fast at our age, except money, kids go through that at the speed of light.

Penny: Are Sandra and Emily about anywhere?

Dad: Sandra is studying the road map of Great Britain trying to locate the whereabouts of her 750cc husband and Emily is touring the tableau of life trying to find a place of employment for her super spouse.

Mum: You look a bit tired, Penny.

Penny: Yes, I am a bit.

Dad: Girls do wear themselves out at her age.

Mum: Do you want a cup of tea, love?

Penny: No, I'm not. . . .

Mum: Not what?

Penny: I'm not holding my liquids, Mum.

Mum: My God, are you trying to tell us something?

Penny: Yes.

Dad: [*Putting his head in his hands*] Don't go into detail. I have a feeling I'm about to be struck by a thunderbolt. . . .

Mum: Penny, look at me, what you telling us. . . .

Penny: Don't be upset. . . .

Mum: You're not trying to say . . . that. . . .

Penny: Yes, Mum, I'm pregnant.

Dad: That phrase, it hangs over a father of daughters like Damocles' flaming sword.

Penny: I'm sorry, Dad.

Dad: Three daughters. Even your two blind sisters missed *that* trap. And you had to spring it on us.

Mum: Barry is it?

Penny: Yes, Mum.

Dad: I thought you kids were intelligent and careful?

Penny: We're also spontaneous, Dad.

Dad: I'm going into the garden. With a bit of luck a stick of rhubarb might reach up and put me out of my misery.

[*He goes*]

Mum: Can you hold a cup of tea now that you've got that off your chest?

Penny: Dad's choked.

Mum: What do you expect. Pregnant at your age . . . does anyone else know?

Penny: Just the school nurse, I've been with her.

Mum: Couldn't you have been with her before it started?

Penny: I wasn't planning anything, Mum.

Mum: Now here's the family trooping in . . . they'll know something's wrong. . . .

Penny: Don't tell them while I'm in the room . . . I'll go out and see Dad.

[*She goes. Enter* **Emily**]

Emily: Mum . . . I have news.

Mum: Don't shock me, I can't stand surprises mid-afternoon.

Emily: Claude has been offered a job; he thinks he's found his rightful niche in society.

Mum: What's he got?

Emily: Personal chauffeur to a Lady Dowager.

Mum: That's nice, where is he now?

Emily: Making an appointment at the fashion designer's.

Mum: For the Lady Dowager?

Emily: No, for himself. She's having a uniform personally designed for him. Well, aren't you excited?

Mum: I'm over the moon and halfway back.

[**Sandra** *enters*]

Sandra: Hello Mum. . . . I've got news for you.

Mum: Couldn't we start a newspaper?

Sandra: I've come out in a skin rash. The doctor says its an allergy.

Mum: What you allergic to?

Sandra: It's just an allergy.

Mum: An allergy isn't a thing in itself like a broken arm. You've got to be allergic to something, like dogs, or grapefruit, or the smell of grass; there's got to be something. What's it like, this rash of yours?

Sandra: Sort of dry, like reptilian.

Mum: You might be allergic to reptiles but there aren't many of them about here.

Emily: Well, Mum, you have had a bundle of news, any more?

Mum: My mundane life trundles on, but Penny dropped a bombshell. . . . She's pregnant. . . .

Emily: Good God.

Sandra: No. Oh where is she?

Mum: Stay where you are, she's out in the garden with her dad.

Scene: **The garden.**

Penny: I've let you down, Dad.

Dad: There's an old expression: 'The man who has children is a hostage to fate'; but the man who has girl children is a hostage to every buck with an arrow in his quiver.'

Penny: I love him Dad.

Dad: Sure you love him, I can't imagine you getting that without love.

Penny: What I mean is, it wasn't just lust.

Dad: Girl, at your age you don't know what lust is; lust comes with the staleness of love and life. Drop of moonlight and innocence crumbles.

Penny: It was this garden that did it, Dad. . . .

Dad: If that's true I'll rotovate it and plant turnips.

Penny: I mean Barry and I found it so romantic.

Dad: This garden was designed for my twilight years, not for your first bloom of spring.

Penny: I'm sure you'd love to nurse your grandson in here, Dad.

Dad: I have two other daughters who can give me grandsons.

Penny: I hope you'll welcome this one in your old manner.

Dad: That isn't the only aspect of it, love. You and Barry are starting out in life; it's like starting a race with ankle chains on, doing it this way.

Penny: So long as we're chained together, Dad, we'll run a good three-legged race.

Dad: There's nothing so exasperating as the optimism of youth.

[*Enter* **Emily** *and* **Sandra**]

Emily: Our Penny, Mum's told us.

Sandra: What have you done?

Emily: He wants seeing to.

Sandra: The stupid fool.

Emily: You can't marry him at your age.

Sandra: He'll have to marry you.

Emily: You'll have to get rid of it.

Sandra: The first of many this'll be.

Emily: What was he thinking of? He's supposed to be intelligent

Sandra: You must have been out of your mind.

Emily: You can't be far gone, thank God it's not too late.

Sandra: You've done it now . . . unless you take that way out.

Emily: It'll be a millstone round your neck.

Sandra: You'll have to sink or swim together.

Penny: What are you on about? Why the hysteria? I'm happy. I'm looking forward to it.

Emily: That's the first flush, that is.

Sandra: You don't realize what it means.

Penny: If this is the first experience of a woman's maturity all I can say is I love the mature life.

[*Enter* **Barry**]

Barry: Penny . . . I've faced your mum.

Dad: Well, that's enough to face for one day. We shan't put you through any more ordeal. Come on, daughters. Back to the house. . . .

Emily: Are you going to *talk* to him.

Sandra: You've got to *say* something, Dad.

Dad: I'm saying nothing yet, these kids are still in the first stages of shell shock. . . .

Emily: Well, I'd like to say something.

[*He ushers them out*]

Penny: Are *you* still in the first stage of shock?

Barry: I feel quite balanced.

Penny: The only shock I'm in is the shock of happiness. Perhaps it's a symptom.

Barry: Perhaps men don't get it.

Penny: Happiness?

Barry: I'm always happy when I'm with you. I don't think anything else has hit me.

Penny: Like what?

Barry: Like . . . all the implications.

Penny: No doubt the grown-ups will hit us with them. Have you told your parents yet?

Barry: No.

Penny: Do you want me to be with you when you do?

Barry: Oh no, I don't want you to be covered in falling plaster when they hit the ceiling.

Penny: Will it be as bad as that?

Barry: I should think it *will* be as bad as that.

Penny: You're not regretting it?

Barry: No, just adjusting to it.

Penny: I suppose you have more adjusting to do. You being the man I mean. You've got to see things differently. Because of the responsibilities. You *are* seeing things differently aren't you? I can see it in your eyes. Even I am different to you already.

Barry: Different . . . but better.

Penny: And the garden, the garden isn't so romantic any more, is it?

Barry: It's different as well, but better again. I see it all with new eyes; I look to see where I would plant the lettuces for salads, and flowers for my little mother-to-be.

Penny: Oh, talk like that Barry and I'm sure your parents won't mind. . . .

Dad: [*To the audience*] The picture of innocence. Perhaps I should alter my theory slightly . . . that marriages of necessity can work first time . . . but there's a long way to run yet. One thing is certain, I can see that Barry is the right man for our Penny . . . so whether she made the choice, or it was thrust on her . . . it seems good.

Scene: **Barry's house.**   *It is very superior, with ducks flying up the wall.*

Father: Son, I hope you realize what you've done to your mother?

Barry: I didn't *try* to do anything to her.

Father: She's having a job to pull herself together.

Barry: She'll get over it.

Father: I was hoping you'd get over it . . . I was hoping that when the full significance of your responsibilities sunk in you'd get over it.

Barry: Over what?

Father: This notion of duty. An obligation to marry the girl . . . it's as old-fashioned as the Crimean medal.

Barry: It's still a good notion to me.

Father: You kids think you're full of new ideas, you think you'll shed a ray of light, you think you'll revolutionize the world, yet when you put a girl up the pod you take the oldest way out and *marry* her. Have you never heard of progress?

Barry: I don't want any so-called progress if it's going to spoil a relationship.

Father: All right, if you won't have progress I'm going to give you the alternative . . . beat a retreat, cut your losses, get out of it. Scram.

Barry: Desert Penny — never. I wouldn't even discuss such a thing when she's coming.

Father: All right, but let's get one thing straight before the jamboree arrives.

Barry: Jamboree — do you mean Penny's parents?

Father: They're all coming, aren't they? Sisters, babies, dogs and flaming oxen.

Barry:　I will not have Penny's family spoken of like that.

Father:　I will speak as I like in my own house . . . and as I say, let me put things straight before the party. . . . You are too young to be a father, and when you are a husband you'll be too old to train to be an architect. You cannot take A-levels when your mind is on nappy rash. You cannot go to University thinking of toddlers. You cannot study in the Bedlam of teething troubles. To be straight, get married and you sink. Stay single and you'll swim. For the first twelve months you'll be happy to be a daddy, for the next twelve years you'll wish you were an architect. For your bliss you'll thank Penny; for your failure you'll curse her.

Barry:　Couldn't I still be an architect?

Father:　No you cannot be an architect and a daddy . . . it's either the drawing board or the ironing board.

Barry:　If you and Mother took Penny and the baby in here and let me stay on at school, and then University. . . .

Father:　Son, I've worked all my life for my pension and my privacy . . . I'm not starting again with your offspring.

Barry:　I see, so there is no way out?

Father:　There is a way out . . . I've looked into it . . . the army.

Barry:　Me. A pongo!

Father:　I'm talking about the modern army. I've looked into it . . . they'll take a lad like you, give you a basic training then send you to a University to study architecture and look after you.

Barry:　And who'll look after Penny and the baby?

Father:　So long as you're serving Queen and country they won't starve.

Barry:　I didn't realize the army took deserters from civilian life. I thought they respected men who stood by duty.

Father:　At your age, son, there is no such thing as ethics.

[*Enter* **Mother**, *trying to control herself*]

Mother: If this motley procession coming down the road is who I think it is I should have put a tea urn on.

Father: You're looking immensely calm, Mother.

Mother: I always look calm when I'm having a nervous break-down; I'm controlling it.

Father: Well, if they're on their way we better get the monkey nuts out.

Barry: Stop that, stop that both of you. That's no way to talk about my future family-in-law.

Mother: I'm sorry, Barry, your father isn't familiar with the mode of addressing council house tenants.

Barry: He should be, he feeds off them.

Mother: What do you mean by that?

Barry: His hire-purchase agreements leech on to their needs.

Father: Not needs, greeds. Everything they see they want, even if they can't pay for it.

Barry: But your advertising company *tempts* them so cleverly.

Father: This is no time for higher economics. You'd better bring your guests in.

[**Barry** *goes*]

Father: Stand by, Mother, you might be losing a son but you're gaining a tribe.

Mother: I am *not* losing a son, I refuse to believe I am losing a son.

Father: You're going to fight, then.

Mother: They're *not* taking my son.

[*She looks grittily but beams when the Larsons enter*]

Mother: Hah, Mr and Mrs Larson, I presume. I'm Barry's mother as no doubt you've heard. This is my husband . . . please settle down . . . get comfortable. . . .

Dad: We're pleased to meet you Mr and Mrs Bellamy. We're very fond of Barry. . . .

Mother: Good . . . we all have his interest and future at heart. . . . Barry darling . . . the tray is all set in the kitchen; bring it in please. . . .

Father: Settle down all.

Mother: And where is the lady of the moment?

Barry: This is Penny, Mother.

Mother: All right, Barry, her parents can introduce me. . . .

Mum: This is our Penny.

Mother: A sensible girl I'm glad to hear. . . . All right Barry, to the kitchen. . . . Now, the rest of your brood Mrs Larson . . . don't be tongue-tied, you're home from home now.

Mum: This is our Emily, and this is her husband Claude.

Mother: Good, do you live with your mother, Emily?

Emily: We have the backroom, but we're optimistic about private accommodation.

Mother: Another council house?

Emily: No, we hope for an apartment in Beaumont Mansions. My husband is starting as chauffeur to Lady Dowager Beaumont.

Mother: Your husband must tell me all about his experiences some time . . . will you?

Claude: Oh. . . .

Emily: I'm sure he will when he's had experience.

Mother: And this one, Mrs Larson?

Mum: This is our Sandra and her husband Smudge.

Father: Is that Smudge's monster motor-bike in the drive?

Smudge: Yamaha 750.

Mother: We don't usually encourage motor-cycles on the rockery, but don't move it now.

Smudge: Wasn't going to.

[**Barry** *enters with the tray*]

Barry: Traffic jam.

Mother: If everyone will find a seat I'll pour. Father, will you open the proceedings?

Father: Er, quite a trip to get out here?

Dad: A Number 37 to the Market Place then we changed stands to get the 144.

Smudge: I came round the Ring Road.

Emily: Claude will soon be very familiar with the routes.

Mum: It was a good bus service though.

Penny: A long wait for the connection.

Smudge: Quite rural, this joint . . . there should be good scrambling in the woods.

Emily: I hope this is the last bus I'll have to go on now Claude is training to drive the Mercedes.

Mum: It was a 'Pay as you enter' bus.

Barry: Good system, those . . . we have them on the school routes.

Dad: I like the old conductor myself, he gives a personal touch.

Sandra: It was a job with the push-chair.

Mum: Nice trip out, though.

All: Oh yes, nice trip out. . . .

[**Mother** *has served the tea*]

Mother: Right, that's enough of the small talk, let's get down to the business in hand . . . what are we going to do about these two young fools?

Barry: Now, Mother. . . .

Dad: We're going to help them.

Mother: Help them . . . they want their bottoms smacked.

Dad: It's happened before, it'll happen again.

Father: It's not happened before in this family.

Sandra: Nor in ours, so don't look at me like that.

Smudge: How's he looking?

Father: I wasn't insinuating anything.

Mother: I repeat, what are we going to do?

Mum: It's up to them, what *they* think they want to do.

Mother: Oh no, they have proved that they are not fit to think for themselves . . . it's up to wiser heads to think for them.

Barry: We can think for ourselves.

Mother: You can only *act* for yourselves, *act* like animals.

Father: Hold up, love, show a little restraint.

Mother: They didn't.

Emily: I must say that's true, they didn't show any restraint.

Sandra: Who's side are *you* on?

Emily: I'm not on anybody's side, but I am on the side of restraint.

Barry: God, there's too much restraint in this house.

Father: And not enough discipline, my lad. But there'll be a drop more from now on.

Barry: A drop more discipline. I'm not a child, I'm going to be a father.

Mother: You needn't be a father if you don't wish, Barry . . .

And Penny needn't be a mother. . . . I've consulted the doctor and he's agreed to stand by.

Penny: Then you can tell him to stand down; I'm going to have my child.

Mother: If you insist on ruining your young life it's your business, and you can make Barry a father, but you can't force him to be a husband.

Dad: There's no *forcing* anywhere along the line.

Sandra: Don't let them sneak out of it.

Father: You can't force Barry to marry at his age.

Mum: What about *her* age.

Mother: Think of his future.

Sandra: Think of the baby.

Smudge: You gotta put the babies first. . . .

Mother: Where will they live? How will they live?

Dad: We can help them.

Mum: It's our responsibility.

Dad: All pull together. . . .

Mum: Co-operate. . . .

Mother: There shall be no help from this house.

Mum: Your own son.

Dad: Your only son.

Mother: If he adopts your family life he is no son of ours.

Dad: But you'll have nothing if he goes.

Mum: Mr Bellamy, *you* would help your boy.

Mother: Father.

Father: I stand by Mother in this.

Sandra: What about standing by the kids?

Father: They made their own mistakes, they must stand by them.

Smudge: Is he looking at you?

Dad: It's the privilege of the young to make mistakes.

Mother: I don't know how you've brought your children up, but mine has been brought up to stand by his own actions.

Mum: We've brought up our kids best we could. . . .

Mother: It shows.

[*A row breaks out*]

Emily: We came here to talk, not to be insulted.

Sandra: Who does she think she is.

Dad: Back to the agenda.

Mother: There seems nothing more to talk about.

Sandra: Some mother *you* are.

Father: That's enough, no more recriminations.

Smudge: Is he looking at you?

Dad: We can't abandon them.

Mother: They mustn't abandon their lives.

Mum: They are our daughter and son.

Mother: I'll have my son, you keep your daughter.

Dad: We're here to advise them.

Mother: They know my advice and I'm willing to stand the bill.

Father: We must come to a decision before it's too late.

Barry: It's not *your* decision . . . it's *our* decision.

Father: What *is* your decision then. Look at your mother, what's she's suffering, how much more she's going to suffer, then tell us your decision.

Barry: What we did, we did together; so, whatever happens we stick together. . . .

Scene: **The Larsons' house.**

Dad: Here am I, heaped in the misfortunes of life. Was there ever such a tormented man? Two daughters blind to the fact that they are married to the wrong blokes; and the third who was my hope, in pod to the right boy.

Mum: So much for your theory, anyway, that girls always marry the wrong man first time round. Barry and Penny look a perfect couple.

Dad: True, but there is still one reservation, they're not married yet.

Mum: Two weeks time we'll be home and dry. And she'll be respectable.

Dad: Home and dry! Mum, the boy is not a creature to be lured and netted. Nor do we want him to do the Honorable Thing. They are disastrous ways to start a marriage.

Mum: But you *do* agree that Penny is going into it with her eyes open. She isn't blinded by love to his faults and failings.

Dad: I think she sees him with clear eyes.

Mum: Good, then your daft theory falls down.

Dad: And as I say, they're not married yet.

[*Enter* **Penny** *and* **Barry**]

Mum: Hello. Put your satchel down, Barry, and have a cup of tea.

Dad: I bet it's funny being at school when you're going to be a dad.

Barry: It seems funny to have my knees under the desk but my father insists I go until the last minute.

Dad: Your father is quite right.

Barry: It's all unnecessary now I'm going on the railways.

Dad: You keep on, learning never went amiss.

Mum: Especially as you don't start on the railways until after the wedding.

Penny: I waited for him at the school gates, the girls gave me quite a fuss when they came out. Miss Dean, the Deputy Head saw me and stopped her car and wound down the window 'We miss you, Penny,' she said. 'You were a good Monitor You were shaping up well.' And I said, in front of all the girls 'I hope to shape up better.' She was very put out, her being a spinster.

Barry: I must say my rating has gone up in the class. It used to be very prestigious to get in the first eleven for cricket, or win a race on Sports Day, or smoke in the sixth form room; but becoming a father beats them all.

Mum: I'm glad you're so happy about it.

Barry: It's never seemed to us an unhappy event at all. And it's very exciting to see it through together.

Penny: That's a nice thing to say.

Barry: I suppose not having brothers and sisters I've never been so closely concerned with anyone before.

Dad: That's true, our lot have been through thick and thin together.

Mum: Sandra taught Penny to swim.

Dad: Emily nursed her through mumps.

Mum: And whenever Sandra had an illness Penny caught it.

Dad: She was bridesmaid at both their weddings.

Mum: They've been through a lot together.

Penny: But nothing like this.

Mum: Oh no, nothing like this.

Dad: How are your mother and father taking it, Barry?

Barry: Mum is pretending it isn't going to happen and Dad is hoping for a last-minute reprieve.

Mum: It can't be very cheerful under those circumstances.

Barry: That's why I like to spend most of my time here, it's *happy*. There are always *people* coming and going and things happening. I don't believe in one-child families any more. I'm going to have lots.

Penny: Hi, hang on, they're not manufactured.

Barry: Oh, we'll develop methods of speeding up the process.

Penny: Listen to this one.

Mum: He can't wait to be a father.

Penny: He was always impulsive.

[*Enter* **Emily** *with* **Claude** *in chauffeur's uniform*]

Emily: Mum, how does he look?

Mum: Lovely.

Dad: He must make the Rolls-Royce look shabby.

Emily: Turn around Claude.

Mum: What a cut.

Emily: Look at that material.

Dad: Does it match the upholstery?

Emily: The Lady Dowager wants him to be a showpiece; when he takes her to Ascot and Henley Regatta and Royal functions.

Dad: She doesn't want *him* as the showpiece, she wants him to make *her* look like a showpiece.

Emily: They set each other off; her class and his style.

Dad: Like Long John Silver and his parrot. I bet her poodle feels a bit put out.

Emily: Mum, we have something else to tell you, haven't we Claude? well, I'll tell them. The Lady Dowager wants him to move into the flat above the garage immediately.

Dad: Can he take a showpiece wife?

Emily: Yes, she's offered me a job as a menial.

Mum: What's a menial?

Emily: I don't know exactly but it means starting at the bottom.

Penny: Your own accommodation!

Emily: So we can start putting out things in tea chests ready to move out; and Claude's suits can be moved in packing cases.

Dad: So, another couple flies from the nest, eh?

Emily: Penny, it means you and Barry can have our room.

Penny: Oh, Dad, you won't have to lose your sitting room after all.

Emily: Come on, Claude, let's start packing. . . .

Penny: Come on, Barry, let's choose a colour scheme. You don't mind if we change things round a bit, Dad?

Dad: Having had my humdrum existence shattered, why should I object to a few minor changes?

[*They go*]

Dad: Emily's blindness is still complete . . . fancy an intelligent, qualified girl like her becoming a menial just to let that stuffed dummy shine. . . . But here is another facet to my theory: a doting wife will humble herself to let her husband sparkle, even if he is a paste diamond like that one. Emily is abasing herself so that he can stand out. A woman will make *any* sacrifice so long as she remains blind to her man's faults. . . .

[*Enter* **Sandra**]

Sandra: Mum.

Mum: Yes, Sandra.

Sandra: I've discovered the cause of my skin disease.

Mum: Oh, that's good. What is the cause?

Sandra: Smudge's tattooes.

Mum: Smudge's tattooes.

Sandra: I'm allergic to tattooes.

Dad: That must be a medical rarity. You'll get in the textbooks.

Sandra: The doctor questioned me about my dreams and found a recurring theme of snakes and feathers and traced them back to the serpents on Smudge's chest and forearms, the eagle on his back. . . . Mum, Dad . . . I think I'm going off him. . . .

Dad: There we are, the first one . . . the blindness of love has lifted.

Sandra: Oh, it's not him . . . it's his tattooes.

Dad: He's always had his tattooes.

Sandra: I was blind to them before.

Mum: Come on, let me see this rash of yours.

Sandra: The doctor said I needn't be an outcast if I join the eczema club.

Dad: That's it, what did I tell you. Suddenly, like the switching on of a light they get a clear vision of their man, then it's all over. He stands there in the glow, a little worm who was once the hero. It is absolutely inevitable, but it is always too late.

[*Enter* **Emily** *with huge cases followed by* **Claude** *with his suit on a coathanger*]

Emily: We're starting to move things over now, Dad. Give Claude a hand or he might crumple his suit.

Dad: That girl is wasting her best years being handmaiden to a dummy. One day she'll realize that *nothing* she has done can make him one bit more intelligent and she'll curse the wasted effort.

[*Enter* **Penny** *and* **Barry** *with sample books*]

Penny: Dad, we thought we'd choose this wallpaper.

Barry: And this is the floor covering to match.

Penny: Do you think they go?

Barry: They're not too similar are they?

Penny: Will you advise us on the hanging?

Barry: Can we get it down before the baby comes?

Penny: Say you think they match.

Dad: They match the way you two match. They blend like you two blend. They suit each other from the ceiling to the floor. Like you two do. You're the perfect little couple you two are.

Penny: Did you hear that, Barry? Kind words coming from the philosopher of matrimony.

Barry: I wish my mother and father had the same philosophy.

Scene: **Barry's home.**   **Mother** *is ticking off the calendar.*

Mother: Five more days to go.

Father: You can't keep ticking your life away.

Mother: Oh my boy. I've tried every sort of restraint, control, appeal but nothing gets through to him.

Father: Your stubborness just made him more stubborn.

Mother: What about *you*. Your tactics have led to nothing.

Father: My tactics as you call them have been positive. I've offered him help, I've offered him *every* alternative. You've just been negative.

Mother: Five days to go. She won't have him. If I have to stand up screaming in church I'll make a last bid to stop it.

Father: Fat lot of good that'll do when they're being married in a registry office.

Mother: A filthy, pokey little registry office with the gypsies, riff-raff and Pakistanis.

Father: Quite reputable people get married in a registry office.

Mother: Not my boy, not my son.

Father: I thought you'd disowned him?

Mother: I tried to withdraw my mother love but it was unnatural, I can see now it was unnatural. It's welling back up, I can feel it, welling up.

Father: Let's prepare for the flood.

Mother: I tried to cut him off, I thought I'd washed my hands of him but now I realize the magnitude of what I've done. I must remedy it . . . there's no time to lose.

Father: You're going to the wedding after all?

Mother: Oh no . . . I've woken up as if out of a cold dream, I'm not going to any wedding, I'm going to offer him something better than a wedding.

[*Enter* **Barry** *with a suitcase*]

Mother: Barry, my boy. Oh Barry, has Mother been cruel? Has she watched you pack your possessions one by one. . . .

Barry: I'm near the end, Mum.

Mother: Oh my boy, my little boy. Taking away his possessions while Mum stood by.

Barry: I thought perhaps you hadn't noticed. Or didn't care.

Mother: Your cricket bat, has that gone? Your first evening suit is now in that council house. The travelling clock your Dad bought you for your birthday, gone . . . are they all gone?

Have you taken all? Those things that meant so much?

Barry: They didn't walk away by themselves, Mum.

Mother: I've been in a daze, oh, a trance, Barry. . . . Don't blame me, I've been in a state of shock. I didn't appreciate how things were. I'd lost my grip on understanding. Barry, I'm all right now.

Barry: Good, Mum, I'm glad you've recovered.

Mother: Thank God it's not too late . . . give me your suitcase.

Barry: Penny is coming for it, Mum.

Mother: No. It belongs here. It all belongs here. You belong here. Oh, to think I nearly let you go through with it.

Barry: Mum, I *am* going through with it.

Mother: No, Barry, don't upset your Mum again . . . say you're not serious, Barry. . . .

Barry: I can't have this . . . I am seriously getting married next week, now face up to it, Mum.

Mother: I can't face up to disaster. You can't do this, Barry. Not Mum. You stay here, Dad will do everything, no one will blame you, say you won't do it.

Barry: For weeks now you've pretended not to care; now you pretend to care; it's all tactics with you, Mum, all a strategy.

Mother: No. It's not tactics, don't say it's tactics, Barry.

Barry: You thought you'd shame me out of it . . . now you're trying the other extreme . . . to blackmail me out of it.

Mother: Oh no, how can you say that? You don't know how I feel. I'm not planning anything. There are no tactics. I don't know how I am. Oh Barry, one minute I'm detached, the next I'm involved. I don't know how I'm going to behave from one time to the next. All I know is I mustn't lose you. Don't throw yourself away Barry, please, my son, please. . . .

Barry: Dad, I can't take this. . . .

Father: You've got to take it. We've all had to take something we didn't like, now it's your turn.

Mother: Barry, please, don't go; delay it if you like, yes, postpone it; give us time to think about it. That's it, we're all more rational now. That's the way to approach it, Barry, please, I'm begging you.

Barry: I am going, Mum.

Mother: I can't envisage what I might do to myself if you go.

Barry: Don't threaten, Mum, don't threaten.

Mother: I'm not threatening, I'm just stating a fact . . . I won't be able to help. myself. . . . Barry, I'm on my knees, your mother is begging, what more do you want. . . .

[*Enter* **Penny**]

Penny: Barry.

Mother: Don't go, don't take it, oh no. It's too final, not everything cleared out, please stay, stay. . . .

[**Barry** *lets go of the case which* **Mother** *hugs*]

Barry: [*To* **Penny**] Let's get out of here. . . .

Scene: **The Larsons' home.**

Dad: One of the phenomena of the women who've married wrong first time round is that they will advise new brides-to-be of the way to make the perfect marriage. And their advice usually implies breaking the husband's spirit for a start. . . .

[**Mum, Sandra, Emily** *and* **Penny** *form a knitting circle.* **Barry** *listens*]

Sandra: You should be teaching *him* how to knit, Penny.

Emily: Oh yes, its all equal rights now.

Mum: Catch Dad knitting, I must say, but he's good at cleaning shoes.

Emily: Modern men are good at things about the house.

Sandra: So I've heard.

Mum: It's the new style husband.

Emily: Nearly every man can turn his hand to cooking nowadays. They all have a speciality dish.

Sandra: Smudge can open a tin. . . .

Mum: Dad makes a good gravy.

Emily: Some men are excellent cooks.

Sandra: Most chefs are men.

Mum: Once a man gets interested it's surprising what he can do.

Emily: It's much more doing things together now.

Sandra: Smudge is only interested in mechanical things.

Mum: Of course the garden is Dad's domain.

Emily: But that's the old-fashioned way. I'm talking about modern men being interested in the woman's side.

Sandra: You'll have to get Barry interested in something, Penny.

Emily: You must find mutual work interest.

Sandra: Now's the time. . . .

Emily: Start as you mean to go on.

Mum: He'll be spending all his time and energy doing a job of work.

Emily: But we *all* do a job of work, not just the men.

Sandra: You'll have to think of helping, Barry, to make an ideal marriage.

Dad: Hi, Barry, come on out here before they have you in harness. . . .

Emily: Don't drag him away, Dad, just when we were making plans for him.

Sandra: Don't start him off on the wrong foot.

Mum: No slipping down to the local with the lads.

Emily: Put your foot down, Penny.

[**Dad** *and* **Barry** *go into the garden*]

Dad: You've got to get away from that lot when they're in a scheming mood.

Barry: I thought it was quite nice.

Dad: Once you've sat through volume three of the Knitting Pattern you're a veteran. Well . . . the great day is getting nearer boy.

Barry: Yes.

Dad: I'm truly sorry you ended up in a bad way with your parents.

Barry: Mum will get over it.

Dad: You must make it good to her as soon as you get the chance.

Barry: I'd make it good to her now if she'd give me the chance.

Dad: Of course you would, you're a good boy.

Barry: Mum just refuses to acknowledge that my marriage is going to happen . . . she's even decorating my room and planning for me to go to University.

Dad: She's had a shock, there's no denying that. Will you miss the experience of University, and Architecture?

Barry: I suppose I will in a way, but I'll be getting other experiences with Penny and British Rail. . . .

Dad: That's the way to look at it, son.

[*Enter* **Penny**]

Penny: Dad, what are you doing with my man?

Dad: Just handing him over, madam.

Penny: Thank you, my man, you may leave.

Dad: Leave? Where can I go? Every room in the house is occupied by a woman and her tongue.

[*He goes*]

Penny: Was it all too much for you?

Barry: No, it was fine. You don't seem to understand I was brought up as an only child . . . I love the gregarious life.

Penny: You could have found the gregarious life somewhere else.

Barry: Like where? The army barracks?

Penny: Or University.

Barry: That wasn't to be.

Penny: It won't always be a full house like this . . . soon it'll be just Mum and Dad, and us and the baby.

Barry: That should be perfect.

Penny: You've had enough for the night. I think you should go home for some peace and quiet.

Barry: There's enough peace and quiet in our house but the peace is very precarious. The atmosphere is as taut as a guitar string.

Penny: All the same, you should go.

Barry: Till tomorrow then.

Penny: And tomorrow, and tomorrow. . . .

[*He goes. Inside,* **Emily**, **Sandra** *and* **Mum** *are talking.* **Dad** *listens on the side*]

Dad: The veil of blindness that films a girl's eyes to her husband's faults sometimes slowly fades away, other times it drops in an instant and she blinks with astonishment at the new vision. . . .

Emily: She'll make a nice bride, our Penny.

Sandra: I wish it was church.

Mum: Yours was a church wedding but Smudge's chapter spoilt it leaning their motor-bikes against the headstones.

Emily: A young honeymoon . . . a pity in way they've spoilt it.

Sandra: Spoilt what?

Emily: You know, the honeymoon, like cutting the cake before the feast.

Mum: Most kids do nowadays.

Emily: Claude and I didn't. Our honeymoon was a period of discovery of one another's bodies. An intimate revelation. Claude looks so beautiful, I think I swooned away for the first three days.

Mum: There'll be a little stranger with them on their honeymoon.

Sandra: You should be thinking of having a family, Emily.

Emily: It's too early yet . . . I just want to keep my body firm and attractive for Claude . . . he's the sort of man who needs a comparable companion.

Dad: I didn't think he ever noticed his companions, he's looking at himself so much. If mirrors were ever abolished he'd die of a broken heart. . . .

[*Enter* **Claude**, *looking beautiful*]

Claude: Em, ready?

Emily: You're rather late.

Claude: Lady Dowager suggested I stay behind and rub down the Mercedes.

Emily: You didn't tell Lady Dowager you were meeting me?

Mum: Will you have a cup of tea?

Claude: Lady Dowager suggested I should have an early night in bed.

Sandra: Have you had a busy day then?

Claude: Lady Dowager's had a very full programme.

Mum: Where did you go?

Claude: Lady Dowager's timetable took her everywhere. . . . Lady Dowager really insisted I should get a beauty sleep, Em . . . shall I wait outside for you?

Emily: Why not phone up and ask Lady Dowager's advice. . . .

Claude: You think I should wait outside?

Emily: Oh yes. I just have to get my handbag, I'll follow you out. . . .

Claude: I'm on duty with Lady Dowager at nine tomorrow and she's told me to get a shine on the car. . . .

[*He goes*]

Emily: He's like a kept lapdog. Why doesn't he use his initiative? Perhaps it'll come with confidence. Will it though? Does it? He still looks lovely in his uniform, there's no denying that. But a man has to be more than a handsome cut if he's to have dignity . . . isn't he? A woman can't live on good looks forever, can she? I mean, beauty is only skin-deep in a marriage, isn't it? Perhaps he'll change. I'd hate to be married to a handsome dummy. Good night all. . . .

[*She goes*]

Dad: I'm afraid Claude's days are numbered. It may take a long time but she's not going to remain satisfied with the state of affairs now she's glimpsed the truth. A woman will slave away for her man so long as she thinks he's worthy; but she'll never give devotion once he's fallen in her sight.

Mum: You're a pessimist about marriage.

Dad: No, dear, a realist.

[*Enter* **Smudge**]

Smudge: What do you mean by leaving the house empty?

Sandra: I've been talking to Mum.

Smudge: I can see you've been talking to Mum . . . But I have a right to come back to a warm welcome after a hard night's riding.

Sandra: I never know when you're coming back.

Smudge: I'm back now, so move. . . .

Sandra: I'm not coming back home tonight, Smudge.

Smudge: You what?

Sandra: The doctor has traced the source of my eczema. Its your tattooes. I can't live with your tattooes. Its like sleeping with a bed of snakes and feathers. Every time you turn over your boa constrictor ripples down your back; your eagle hovers on your chest and when you throw your arm around me I'm choked by a python, not to mention the rattlesnake on your wrist. . . .

Smudge: You are married to me and my tattooes.

Sandra: Please, Smudge, I can't bear it . . . let me stay here.

Smudge: You're coming back. Where's the baby?

Sandra: In the pram, in the passage.

Smudge: Right, he's coming back with me for starters.

Sandra: You can't take him . . . there's no way to carry him.

Smudge: I'll sling him across the petrol tank, baby . . . if you want him you better follow.

[*He goes*]

Sandra: Oh God, Mum, I can't bear him . . . he's so repulsive . . . I can't bear his physical presence.

Mum: If you want your baby it looks as though you'll have to.

[*There is a roar of the motor-bike*]

Smudge: You coming then?

Sandra: My God, he's doing it, he's doing it. . . . Wait. . . .

[*She rushes off*]

Dad: It's ironical. It was the tattooes and motor-bike she fell in love with. In the old days she considered him a walking work of Art. Now her eyes are open he's more reptile than Rembrandt. . . .

Penny: Is it always like this, Dad? Is it inevitable?

Dad: I'm not saying it's inevitable but it's almost deadly certain that girls rush into marriage and marry the wrong feller, for the wrong reason, first time round.

Penny: What is the wrong reason?

Dad: Love. Blind love, the worst reason in the world for getting married. Better to marry for money, for security, for fame, for friendship, but not for love first time round, it's too dazzling. The heat of love obscures things; puts a haze between the girl and her man . . . and when the love-glow lifts she's faced with the grim, ugly, reality and can rarely live with it. But I tell you, my dear, you are doubly lucky because you have a double vision, you're seeing Barry with *your* eyes, and with *my* eyes. . . . And it can tell you . . . he's the right man for you.

Penny: Thanks, Dad. . . .

Scene: **The Larsons' house, later.**   **Barry** *is reading.* **Penny** *enters.*

Barry: Penny, I didn't expect you.

Penny: Crept up on you unawares.

Barry: Trying to catch me out?

Penny: I'd never do that, you know.

Barry: There's nothing to discover.

Penny: I know. We don't keep things from one another. It's one of Dad's old adages, 'Never hide anything from those you love because they're sure to find out. . . .'

Barry: And disillusion set in.

Penny: What you reading?

Barry: Never hide anything.

Penny: [*Reading*] 'The fundamentals of architecture. . . .' Are you going to miss Architecture?

Barry: I can always read it up, as a hobby. . . .

Penny: Please don't look so wistful.

Barry: No, I'm not wistful, am I?

Penny: You've had a few shocks.

Barry: We've both had shocks.

Penny: I'm going to give you one more.

Barry: Serious?

Penny: Deadly serious.

Barry: There's nothing wrong with baby, or you?

Penny: No, mother and child are thriving on it . . . brazen hussies.

Barry: Then what is it?

Penny: I'm not going through with our marriage.

Barry: You're what?

Penny: I'm not marrying you, Barry.

Barry: But . . . our baby . . . you said you wanted the baby.

Penny: Oh, I want the baby all right, and I'll have it. The greatest miracle in the world is creation and I'm not going to butcher it.

Barry: Then we must marry to do it justice.

Penny: Let's cut out words like justice, duty, responsibility.

Barry: Love then.

Penny: Love is good. But I'd prefer to turn you away for love. Marriage can only wear love down. I can love you without a wedding, so walk away. I'll watch your career and life with interest, and devotion.

Barry: You're doing this for me, aren't you? You feel as though you owe it to me because you halted my career.

Penny: You halted *my* career as well.

Barry: You mean to have the baby adopted?

Penny: No, I mean to keep my baby, but I can be a mother without being tied to the father.

Barry: Penny, I *want* to marry you.

Penny: I'm sure you do now, but I'm turning you down.

Barry: Give me a reason.

Penny: I don't want to put fingers on certain parts of our relationship; I don't *want* to analyse the happiness we've had. But as I feel it, if we get married it is the result of our Little Mistake. No matter how successful it turns out all of our life and struggle will have sprung from that youthful mistake. We will be welded together . . . because our seeds joined together. But suppose we don't treat it as a mistake, suppose we believe it happened to me the way things *should* happen — as a development of life, the way the rain falls, and the grass grows; then it will remain a fertile fruitful part of my life. That's how I want it.

Barry: I shall never stop offering to marry you.

Penny: Oh, don't say that *offer*. It sounds so dutiful.

Barry: I shall never stop asking you to marry me then.

Penny: That will be wonderful. To think I will always be courted. Always have a suitor. But I'm warning you, I only want a *successful* man as my suitor, I don't want to be courted by a failure. In five years' time a young qualified architect will be wooing me; and then a rising successful young man climbing in his profession; then the mature builder who has designed masterpieces will be asking for my hand ... then perhaps a silver-haired, honoured, famous man. Always there to court me. And I shall always have something to give him.

Barry: What's that?

Penny: Free, boundless, undutiful love. Now please go your way, I'm going mine.

[*They part*]

Epilogue (optional)

Dad: Unlike most brides Penny passed her arranged wedding day with complete calm. She felt happy because she was at one with life. She was happy that, after the birth of her baby, new adventures of life and possibilities of interest would arise. She was happy that the boy she loved was following his own life; every bit of his success was her success, every portion of his happiness was a share of her happiness. And I had a new element to my marriage theory. . . . 'A girl always falls in love with the right boy first time, but it is inevitably too early, and she too innocent for marriage.'

The End

Never Right, Yet Again

Peter Terson

Characters

Duncan Stoner, referred to as Dad
Shona Stoner, referred to as Mum
Kirby, their elder son, aged 20
Wendy, their daughter, aged 18
Ian, their younger son, aged 16
Katie, a friend of Wendy
Judy, Kirby's girlfriend

First performed by the National Youth Theatre at the Round
House Downstairs, 18 August 1977

Never Right, Yet Again

Scene: **The Stoners' House.** **Mum** *and* **Dad** *are sitting and reading. Although they are in their early middle age, both are young and vital.*

Mum: Listen to this. . . .

Dad: My life seems to have been a series of snippets read out of your newspapers.

Mum: Don't you want to hear it?

Dad: Go on.

Mum: Its one of these Gallup polls with young people.

Dad: We can do without that.

Mum: 'A cross-section of young people in Technical Colleges, factories and schools of further Education were asked what they thought of their parents' sex lives.'

Dad: No wonder we're a decadent society.

Mum: But the results were rather surprising: 'Adolescents revealed a naive outlook at the sex lives of their parents. It was shown that 90 per cent thought that parents over the age of forty had passed sex.'

Dad: In the 1930s the world had Einstein's theory of relativity, in the 1970s we have this. Is that not remarkable progress in the field of mathematics.

Mum: 'Fifteen per cent of the young people reluctantly admitted that their parents may indulge in some sort of sexual activity a few times a month, or at Christmas or other festive occasions.'

Dad: Hang out the balloons, I'm getting randy.

Mum: 'It was concluded that young people refused to acknowlege their parents as actively sexual people.' Doesn't that surprise you?

Dad: Not a bit of it. in my experience as a family man young people refuse to acknowledge parents at all except as mechanical diggers out of wallets or forkers out of cash.

Mum: Well they're engaged in their own affairs.

Dad: No, they're obsessed with their own selves.

Mum: I better not leave this lying around.

Dad: Oh don't worry, they'd refuse to even acknowledge that in cold print. Young people have a cut-out system that isolates them from any human contact with their parents' needs or feelings.

Mum: Our kids wept buckets when you broke your ankle falling off the ladder.

Dad: That was just shock reaction. Next day they started a giggle that was to last a fortnight. When parents conceive, they form their own strangers.

Mum: Don't say that after all these years.

Dad: But it's all these years that have taught me to face the fact. As a father I have no right in their eyes to exist as an emotional being. And of course *we* encourage them. From an early age we pretend that only *they* exist; from pottie training to first erection we shelter them from the fact that *we* go to the bog and have sexual intercourse. We applaud even their mistakes to give them courage. From the first steps and toddles we put on a mask of parental interest and earnestness that eventually persuades them that we don't exist in *ourselves.*

Mum: Perhaps *you* should have run the Gallop poll.

Dad: I could have come up with the conclusions without giving them the vote.

Mum: If parental role has been such a self-defacing strain you can begin to come out; ours are safely out of childhood and on the edge of the nest, ready to fly off.

Dad: Having soiled it for twenty years.

Mum: No need for this self-mockery, you've been a good dad.

Dad: I've been a good actor. Spurring them on, feigning interest, effacing myself.

Mum: It's part of being a father.

Dad: But its such a *long* part. I want to show them I am myself; strip off the mask; reveal myself naked, cry, 'Look at me, pinch me, I feel, I fart.'

Mum: I'm sure they know the last well enough.

Dad: And what about the other items?

Mum: They're *your* children. Some kids can take things, others can't; you should know them well enough.

[*Pause*]

Dad: I suppose *you're* anticipating the grandma years?

Mum: I'm not *anticipating*, but with our Kirby at twenty and courting strong they might be thrust upon me.

Dad: I'm not going through yet another act, the beaming old grandpa role.

Mum: It's inevitable, its the Seven Ages of Man.

Dad: Can't we slip another one in the cycle somewhere? The return of Youth Age? You see, it's all too much of a sacrifice. To hide your *real* self for the sake of the children; to be the blank face behind the pipe; the firm hand on the end of the long rein. I mean, I admit, I've been very good at it: old Dad, the amiable buffon; old Dad who intervenes when all else is lost; old Dad who is very rarely right but wrong again; old Dad, *never right yet again.* I don't *want* to be expressionless Dad any more . . . I'd like to be *me.* Taken by them as other people take me, *Duncan.* . . . Flesh and blood Duncan.

Mum: You're flesh and blood Duncan at work, and down the pub.

Dad: Forget it, I'm at my old game of batting my head against a brick wall.

Mum: No, let's have it out.

Dad: We've been having it out between ourselves for twenty years, we just need to have it out with *them* for a change.

Mum: Well, if you're going to begrudge your role as a father then I think you should help yourself and. . . .

Dad: Hold it . . . here is a return to the nest. 'Hello, Mum, dinner on? Hello, Dad, not at work?'

[**Kirby**, *dressed in engineer's overalls and carrying a bag, enters*]

Kirby: Hello Mum, dinner on? Hello Dad, not at work?

Mum: Can't you smell it?

Dad: I just sit about the house.

Kirby: Have I time for a bath?

Dad: Going out, son? Not that it's any of my business.

Kirby: Mum, I couldn't find a clean shirt this morning.

Mum: You didn't need one this morning.

Kirby: But I'm going out tonight.

Mum: You'll find one tonight, I put them in your drawer this afternoon.

Kirby: You might have said.

Dad: You are a bit unreasonable, Mum, with your laundry habits.

Kirby: Have you been loafing about all afternoon, Dad?

Dad: I only got in half an hour ago.

Kirby: What a cushy job.

Dad: Ridiculous, isn't it. And I get paid.

Kirby: You're *always* at home.

Dad: Correction, if I may, I *always look* as if I'm at home.

Kirby: You always seem at home when I'm about.

Dad: True. But when you're *not* about I'm on my morning insurance round; then I do my afternoon calls when you're not about; collect three evenings a week when you're out and help out in the bar of the Three Tuns at weekends and functions.

Kirby: What a job.

Dad: I don't know how it works but I've managed to bring up a family for twenty years.

Kirby: Just!

Dad: Do I detect discontent? When you leaving?

[**Kirby** *goes*]

Mum: I hate it when you take that attitude. Pure sarcasm.

Dad: Oh, did I use that weapon? Break the Geneva Convention, did I? No mustard gas or sarcasm?

Mum: Asking them when they're leaving, it's like pushing them into the deep end when they're hesitating over the plunge.

Dad: That's how I learned to swim.

Mum: And we all know what *your* confidence hides.

Dad: No, you and I know what my confidence hides. They don't.

[**Kirby** *re-enters, without his overalls. He goes to his bag*]

Dad: Kirby, loathe as I am to ask, what on earth do you bring home in that bag?

Kirby: Few things.

Dad: From work?

Kirby: Bit of tat.

Dad: Like spare pipe, scrap metal, few brass bolts, that sort of thing?

Kirby: Things like that.

Dad: My son, you're an apprentice engineer not a shoplifter.

Kirby: Everybody does it at work nowadays.

Dad: I don't.

Kirby: What's worth having in your stupid job?

[*He goes*]

Dad: What *is* worth having in my stupid job? Integrity, my son, that's what. Does it never cross his mind that he's betraying me?

Mum: Betraying?

Dad: When he left school I went to the factory and *begged* them to take him on; I wore my best suit and carried his O-level results in my briefcase. I was giving an impression of loyalty and honesty, not sponsoring a petty thief.

Mum: I'm sure it's a recognized thing among the men.

Dad: But if he's going to accept *their* moral code anything can become the recognized thing. He's had enough equipment out of that firm these years to service Concorde.

Mum: It's only scrap.

Dad: He *sells* it as scrap, but in reality it's very expensive stuff;

you could sell the Crown Jewels for scrap if you melted them down. Those brass bolts are very special, specifically built for the job, specified by engineering designs, valuable to the firm, difficult to replace — but he pops them into the melting pot at the scrapyard for twenty pence a time.

Mum: If you're going to start before dinner. . . .

Dad: I'm sorry, I was being unreasonable again. Well done, Kirby, my son and heir, well stolen.

Mum: Do you know what I think?

Dad: What?

Mum: All this pilfering that he does, I've got a theory it's all pyschological; it's a call of despair at working conditions; a cry of frustration against unions; a voice raised in protest.

Dad: I've got another theory. I think its pure greed.

Mum: Oh well, if you're going to be like that.

[*She goes*]

Dad: I have a feeling I *am* going to be like that.

[*Enter* **Ian** *with a bang*]

Dad: Hi Ian, why don't you try opening that door before you come in?

Ian: I'm practising my transcendental passage.

Dad: Pity it leaves bootmarks on the door.

Ian: Have I still got a mum?

Dad: Oh no, son, when you come in the back door she automatically pops out the front. It's a reflex action like a cuckoo clock.

Ian: [*Calling*] Mum, do you happen to be coming out this way with a pair of buttered scones?

Dad: You take a long time to get back from school, Ian.

Ian: It's the most interesting part of the day, studying the passing parade of life.

Dad: Shouldn't you be studying the passing parade of education as well?

Ian: Dad, one of the things I've always admired about you is your liberal attitude to learning.

Dad: Like to think I'm vaguely progressive.

Ian: Here's my staid, old-fashioned school report.

Dad: I thought there was something coming.

Ian: Get it in perspective Dad . . . and whatever they say in there note how neat and tidy I've left the envelope.

Dad: What a rare talent. . . .

[*Enter* **Mum**]

Ian: Hello, Mum, your smiling gourmet is back . . . what's in the tin?

Mum: Currant buns.

Ian: That should keep the pecker up as the chicken said. Better give Dad a bit of rising pastry to avoid that sinking feeling.

Mum: School report?

Ian: Do you want me to leave the room while you weep into your tea?

Dad: Son, far be it for me to criticize your attitude to school, but when it says, 'He likes to act the fool,' or, 'He plays the clown,' wouldn't you be better off with Billy Smart's Circus?

Ian: The whole world needs the laughs, Dad.

Dad: Oh, agreed, but it doesn't *pay* for them. Do you want to see this joke sheet, Mum?

Mum: Bad as that, is it?

Dad: That's the best bit. 'If he had as much serious endeavour as he has buffoonery he may make progress.'

Ian: Dad, there is such a pile of neurotic geniuses at school waiting to join the struggle in the outside world, you should be grateful that I'm thick.

Dad: It doesn't say *thick* anywhere, it says *stupid*.

Mum: All this acting the fool, Ian.

Ian: Anyway, I've told the Head I'm leaving school and he wants to see Dad.

Dad: I'll put on my false nose and tell him it runs in the family.

Mum: Clowning won't get you anywhere Ian.

Ian: All right, I repent. I'm going up to my bedroom. When you want me for tea knock on the Big Top.

[*He goes*]

Mum: Life's all clowning to him.

Dad: He'll find when he has to take it seriously he's laughing on the other side of his face.

Mum: Mind you, he's a good-natured boy.

Dad: Oh yes, it's the other side of the coin from Kirby; trouble is, it's the same bad penny.

Mum: Now, now, your own sons.

Dad: Well, all this vacuous clowning and deadening sullenness.

Mum: Do you know what I think about Ian's clowning? I think he acts the fool because he's under the shadow of Kirby.

Dad: Couldn't it be that he's just daft?

Mum: I know he's the flibbertigibbet of the family but his development has always been obstructed by big brother Kirby.

Dad: Couldn't we ask big brother Kirby to leave and we'll all develop?

Mum: Don't start *that* again.

[*Enter* **Kirby**]

Kirby: Is it all right if I bring Judy home to tea?

Dad: Well, we'll be glad.

Kirby: Mum?

Mum: Yes, Kirby, when?

Kirby: Tomorrow.

Mum: That's sudden.

Kirby: I've been going out with her for three years.

Mum: Yes, I know, but it's a sudden decision to bring her home.

Kirby: It's taken Dad such a long time to put a new carpet down in the front room.

Dad: Kirby, I didn't realize. Honest. We'd love to meet your girl. If you'd give me a list of fixtures and fittings you'd like changed I'll do it to create the right impression.

Kirby: I feel embarrassed, bringing anybody to this dump. . . . One other thing . . . it's an engagement tea, all right?

Mum: That's all right with me . . . and your Dad, I'm sure.

[**Kirby** *goes*]

Dad: Congratulations.

Mum: Well, engaged.

Dad: Now he's a social phenomenon beyond my comprehension. I have brought up my eldest son with a fairly liberal hand; guided him easily through the permissive age; made myself available for advice and encouragement, and yet he darkly, defiantly reveals the secret, 'I am to be engaged,' as if I'm going to stamp on it with my Victorian boot.

Mum: Still, if Ian sees big brother's engaged and about to go off it might allow him to bloom.

Dad: Bloom into what? A daft daisy or a barmy buttercup?

Mum: I think when he sees Kirby is going he will prepare to take over the man's role in the house.

Dad: Good, where do I come in? Or shall I just stay as doormat?

Mum: You have Wendy; you're *her* guiding image. She's coming down from College tomorrow by the way, and bringing a friend, so Duncan, *act normal*. . . .

[*She goes*]

Dad: Act normal! The one thing I haven't been able to do for twenty years is act bloody normal.

Scene: **The following day.**   **Dad** *is fiddling with his scrapbook, the glue and scissors.* **Mum** *enters.*

Mum: It'll be nice, Wendy bringing a friend home from College.

Dad: Yes, there might be a fragment of intelligent conversation between the walls.

Mum: She comes from a good home.

Dad: We all do when we're somewhere else.

Mum: She's His and Geog.

Dad: She's what?

Mum: Her subjects, History and Geography.

Dad: I hate these abbreviations. I thought you said, she's pissed on grog.

Mum: Very funny.

Dad: Depends on my audience. How long's she stopping?

Mum: Just as it suits them.

Dad: That'll make a change. Putting themselves first.

Mum: That's enough of that.

Dad: Where's she sleeping? Boys moving out I hope?

Mum: I've made the twin beds up in Wendy's room.

Dad: Push them together and let young Lesbos bloom.

Mum: Don't let them hear you talk like that!

Dad: They've never heard me talk my true natural voice in their lives. Were they to get but a glimpse of the fantasia which is my sexual self they would wilt.

Mum: Were they to get a glimpse of your erotic collection they would wilt.

Dad: No, they would put it down to Dad's senility and dirty little second childhood.

Mum: All the same I hope they never find it.

Dad: Don't worry, its under lock and key with my insurance policies, to be burnt at my death.

Mum: Dad's little art collection.

Dad: I must say I get a fairy-tale delight harbouring my casket of erotica within these four walls. It's like harbouring my genie among the enemy. To take it out at night when they are occupied with boring pursuits like discotheques and pop scenes and lift up the lid to release the magic fairies of delight.

Mum: Yes, but don't talk about it in broad daylight. It's a nocturnal magic.

Dad: It benefited *you* and your sex life.

Mum: We benefited one another.

Dad: But it's the man who has to kindle the flame of passion and develop the stimulus.

Mum: And of course the woman *does* nothing.

Dad: Look. . . .

Mum: Look nothing, we've had it all before.

Dad: Oh, what's the use of having a conversation. . . .

Both: Unless you agree with everything I say.

[*Enter* **Ian** *with a bang. He is carrying several cases*]

Ian: Sis has arrived.

Dad: You look great carrying bags, Ian; you ought to try it for your Mum sometime.

Ian: They came in a little MG. Sis was with this super bird parking, and I went up behind her and said, 'Carry your bag, miss?' and touched her bottom. She nearly swallowed the parking meter.

Dad: Your sense of humour will be the death of traffic wardens.

Mum: I hope Wendy explained who you were?

Ian: She said she saw the family resemblance. Between my face and Wendy's bum.

Dad: Ian, when I was a boy. . . .

Ian: Didn't know you were; I thought you were hatched out old?

Dad: My grandmother had an expression that she used on me to such devastating effect that I swore I would never use it on my children; nevertheless there was a lot of truth 'in it, viz, 'Fools should be seen but not heard.'

Ian: They were amateur fools.

Mum: Why don't you give up, Dad? Throw in the towel.

Dad: After twenty rounds? Never.

Ian: Here they come. Fanfare. Bah, bah, be-bah.

[**Wendy** *and* **Katie** *enter*]

Wendy: Hello, Dad, you old cheat.

Dad: What have I done this time?

Wendy: I don't know but you're guilty until proved innocent. Mum, this is Kate.

Mum: Hello Kate, you're His and Geog.

Wendy: Oh God, Mum, that's the worst greeting since 'Dr Livingstone, I presume.'

Mum: Just leave everything where it is, girls, I'll make a cup of tea.

Dad: When in doubt, rush out.

Mum: They'd like a cup. . . . You had a nice drive down?

Katie: Fine, thank you.

[**Mum** *goes*]

Dad: It's a fact of your Mum's existence that when she meets somebody new in *my* presence her level of small talk drops to a flustered two centimetres; but as soon as I'm absent she plunged into Dostoevskian depths with her new friends. It's true, you'll see.

Wendy: Perhaps she has shallows in which she sports with you, and an ocean on which she swims alone.

Ian: Anyway Dad, you have your scrapbook.

Dad: Oh, here we go; watch this, Kate, and listen. Here is Dad being *set* up like an Aunt Sally.

Wendy: [*Fondly*] A very nice Aunt Sally. Dad has a scrapbook, Katie.

Ian: Kept it for twenty years.

Wendy: A pageant of History.

Ian: A social record.

Wendy: Started with his marriage certificate.

Ian: Ends with his death certificate. Lines the walls of his room with the volume.

Ian: Had to get planning permission to erect such a monument.

Wendy: He is the Samuel Pepys of our block.

Ian: Everything goes in there from bootlace wrappers to bus tickets.

Wendy: Receipts and bills.

Ian: Betting slips and birthday cards.

Wendy: Pressed flowers and tea-bags.

Ian: He had to have a bumper volume for Coronation Year.

Wendy: But he's *very lovable* with his scissors and paste.

Ian: His fingers have been stuck together since we've known him.

Katie: Don't you *write* in it?

Wendy: Write? Oh no, he doesn't *write* in it.

Ian: Too much like hard work.

Wendy: He hasn't got the creative urge to *write*.

Ian: He's strictly a scissors and paste man.

Katie: It's a pity you don't write.

Dad: I'm not a literary man . . . but despite the scoffers, objects, like words, can stir the memory and kindle the imagination.

Wendy: Whooo, beautifully put, Dad.

Ian: The philosopher strikes.

[*Enter* **Mum**]

Mum: Come on then, Dad, clear this lot away.

Katie: Mr Stoner, I hope something of me goes in your scrapbook.

Dad: We'll have to see if any little items create a firm impression.

Mum: All for tea?

Ian, Wendy: Yes, please.

Mum: Visitors first. . . . Katie?

Katie: Yes, please.

Ian: How do you like it, Katie, weak or strong?

Katie: As it comes.

Ian: With or without?

Katie: With one.

Ian: Long or short?

Katie: Long or short?

Ian: You've heard of a long drink, you've heard of a short drink, do you want your tea drink long or short?

Wendy: Humour him.

Katie: Long, please.

[Ian *pours from a height*]

Wendy: Standard joke, it's a tradition.

Ian: It never fails to please.

Wendy: So it shouldn't, you've been rehearsing it for years.

Ian: I like to think it's one of my polished gems.

[Kirby *enters*]

Kirby: You back then?

Wendy: Do you mind?

Ian: We've suffered, horribly.

Kirby: So does my record pile, while I'm away.

Wendy: That's Ian.

Ian: It isn't, I just had the Rolling Pins and that was scratched.

Kirby: You have them all.

Ian: Wendy, you check . . . he's had Frank Sinatra's 'Romantic Mood' since he started courting.

Wendy: That'll be worn smooth.

Dad: Hi, I hate to interrupt this high-level flow of conversation but shouldn't you introduce your visitor?

Wendy: You're so old-fashioned, Dad. They've got each other's vibes without the formal ceremony.

Dad: I thought the curt acknowledgement might not come amiss, you do it when the cat comes in.

Wendy: She can take it all in, can't you, Kate?

Katie: I think I've sussed out who's who.

Dad: Just in case you've missed the family tree, that's Kirby, the eldest.

Katie: Hi, Kirby.

Kirby: Come here often?

Ian: Excuse our old retainer in the corner but, he's never emerged since the footman lost his voice.

Kirby: We usually tie a label round his neck when strangers arrive.

Wendy: He's spent so much time trying to get into the dialogue he talks to himself.

Ian: The only invitation he's had is to keep silent.

Kirby: Careful what you say, Katie, or he'll press you in his scrapbook.

Ian: The mute record.

Dad: Note, how I weather the storm.

Kirby: Hi Mum, are the sleeping arrangements altered?

Ian: No, Dad's staying with us.

Kirby: I've got a new LP you can listen to, Wendy, if you've got nothing to do.

Wendy: Might as well. Coming, Kate?

Katie: Might as well.

Wendy: Nothing else to do round here.

[*They go*]

Dad: [*Calling*] Don't bother about the dishes, we'll wash up.

Mum: It's only a handful.

Dad: It'll be a sinkful by tonight; then you'll be sorry you weren't firm from the start.

[**Wendy** *re-enters*]

Wendy: Dad. [*Kisses him*] In case I forgot first time. That's to say I love to see you.

Dad: You didn't forget first time.

Wendy: [*Kissing him again*] That cancels it, then.

[*She dashes out*]

Dad: What was all that about?

Mum: That girl's got something on her mind.

Dad: How do you know?

Mum: I know. You'll see. It'll come out.

Dad: Not pregnant is she?

Mum: I said on her mind.

Dad: Phew, I don't care what's on her mind so long as it isn't in the oven.

[*Enter* **Katie**]

Katie: Did I leave a small hold-all?

Dad: Er, yes, over there.

Katie: Good, there's something I want in it.

Dad: What's the label?

Katie: Label? Oh, I flew to France last year.

Dad: May I?

Katie: Of course.

[*He takes the label and puts it in his scrapbook*]

Scene: **Later that afternoon.** **Dad** *is sitting down.* **Mum** *enters with preparations for a classy tea.*

Mum: Well, I don't know what Kirby expects to show his girl but I've done my best.

Dad: Florence Nightingale at Balaclava would have been impressed with this lot of bullshit.

Mum: I suppose he wants to show the standard he's used to.

Dad: Standard he's used to. When did we last have the silver spoons, paper doilies and Micky Mouse Meringues?

Mum: Bit of a fling.

Dad: Her home must be a four-star home with Egon Ronay cooking.

Mum: It might soften Kirby when he sees her in his own home background.

Dad: All these standards he's rejected and abused all these years are now to be showpieces.

Mum: Perhaps he's come round to them.

Dad: What if I described it to her as he's described it to me — 'Welcome to our mortgaged hovel,' 'Take a seat in the soup kitchen,' 'Join the trough.'

Mum: Children are always embarrassed by their home.

Dad: So are we all but only they are allowed to say so. . . .

Mum: [*Ominously*] You're allowed to say so, Duncan . . . if that's how you feel.

Dad: [*Guilt*] I'm sorry. I take that back. . . .

Mum: I'd hate to think you weren't happy with our home even if you have doubts about our life. . . .

Dad: Total surrender, I love it . . . back in the family habit quick. . . . Where are Wendy and Kate?

Mum: Shopping. Last refinements for tea.

Dad: Oh, serviettes? Glacé cherries and chocolate leaves?

Mum: I thought with being her age-group they'd understand her taste.

Dad: Oh, I think I understand her taste. From the way Kirby has pilfered for four years, it's . . . anything expensive.

Mum: You're only young once.

Dad: How you smother your frustration with platitudes astonishes me.

Mum: No use letting frustration rule you. As you never stop telling me.

Dad: I've released some of yours in our time.

Mum: And your own.

Dad: You've got something on your mind.

Mum: You can read me like a book.

Dad: No, but I know when you're a closed book.

Mum: It's Wendy . . . it's in confidence . . . I'm not to tell you, mind.

Dad: Agreed, what's up?

Mum: She has an infatuation.

Dad: Its always ominous when you call it an 'infatuation'.

Mum: It's with her psychology tutor.

Dad: Thát's convenient.

Mum: He's fifty-three years of age and got teenage children of his own.

Dad: When does he draw his pension? We might all get a slice.

Mum: Aren't you worried?

Dad: She's been having infatuations with old men since she went to high school. I worried myself sick over the caretaker but by the time she got through her education to the schools career adviser I was hardened.

Mum: She wants to tell you in her own time.

Dad: Great. She won't mis-time her entrance.

Mum: You shouldn't be glib, there's a lot of the onus can be laid at your door.

Dad: Oh yes, I wish the council had a refuse collection for responsibilities, I'd fill them up with my garbage.

Mum: Something she said, let slip, put a whole new light on the affair. She said, about this lecturer, 'He's got Dad's sense of comfort.'

Dad: Listen, when you've studied psychology for three years like she has, that's not a slip, it's a well-planted bombshell.

Mum: She was always over-fond of you.

Dad: Incest you mean?

Mum: Before she went to high school she was always coming into our bed in the small hours and it was usually me who ended up in the cot.

Dad: Well, I could hardly curl up in it. Not with Andy Pandy and bloody Teddy.

Mum: You have to take responsibility for what you do to your children.

Dad: That's not fair, they don't take responsibility for what they've done to me . . . I could say to each one separately, 'Look. . . . .'

Mum: Well, don't, here's one of them now.

Dad: It's Ian. He's early, he must be driven in by the rain.

[**Ian**, *looking thoughtful, enters*]

Ian: Hi, Mum, it's the introductory tea today, isn't it?

Mum: Yes. But don't make a pig of yourself.

Ian: Not even a tiny grunt?

[**Mum** *goes out.* **Ian** *glances at* **Dad**]

Ian: I'll be ever so good, I'll put my tails in curlers.

[*He gets no response.* **Ian** *takes out a music stand and puts paper on it. He pretends to play the guitar while glancing at* **Dad**]

Dad: Nice tune that, Ian.

Ian: Yes, but I think this guitar has had it.

Dad: Why do you say that?

Ian: I think the central heating has warped it.

Dad: That could be true of a lot of things.

Ian: I think I better sell it off.

Dad: Hah, so that's it.

Ian: Buy a scrambler, I'm dying for a scrambler.

Dad: You were dying for a guitar two years ago.

Ian: You grow out of them.

Dad: Untouched.

Ian: It'll look good in the advert: 'Guitar, virtually unused'.

Dad: But I use it.

Ian: But it's *mine*, isn't it?

Dad: Ian, when you were thirteen the world was going to collapse if you couldn't get a guitar. Your already tottering school work crumbled; your spirits hit a dangerous low, and you didn't sleep at nights because you'd heard Donovan or somebody sing 'Send in the Clouds' to guitar. So, for the *general* state of your health and general well-being (I'm just stating facts, mind you) I bought you a guitar and the Golden Tutor Book 1; which you agreed to pay back with sundry errands and jobs which were rarely completed. However, I must say you tackled the guitar with a worthy concentration, for two weeks. Then you packed it back in its case and never got it out again.

Ian: Well, it was boring, all that learning.

Dad: All that *effort*. However, Dad, being the thrifty, economical old 'Waste not, want not' that he is, took out the aforesaid instrument and opened the Guitar Tutor and now after two and a half years he is on Book 4 and tackling Sor's Etude and Carcassis's Study in A, quite nicely . . . and *I'm* damned if it'll leave the house.

Ian: Want to buy it off me?

Dad: I'll run errands and do jobs about the house like you did.

Ian: Thanks, Dad, you're a real pal.

Dad: That guitar is part of the fixtures and fittings.

Ian: Great . . . you can pinch my stamp album while you're about it.

Dad: I would do but you swopped the stamps for marbles. . . .

[**Ian** *goes.* **Mum** *enters*]

Mum: Have you upset Ian?

Dad: He wanted to sell the guitar.

Mum: He's always been swopping and changing things.

Dad: He's like the Exchange and Mart, that kid.

Mum: What does he want *this* time?

Dad: A scrambler.

Mum: But I thought you were going to get him one for his birthday?

Dad: I was; big secret, wasn't it? Well, he's jumped the queue, he can have a tiepin instead.

Mum: Oh, dear. . . .

[*She goes*]

[**Katie** *enters, carrying the shopping*]

Katie: Hello.

Dad: Hello, Katie, where's your little pal?

Katie: Wendy? Oh, walking, just walking.

Dad: Left you, has she? Well, sure you'll not be without things to do.

Katie: I'll take the shopping in to Mrs Stoner and then come back and talk to you.

Dad: Oh, yes, I was just going out into the garden . . . try to make sense with the rhubarb.

Katie: I'll come out into the garden, too. If that's all right with you. Is that all right with you?

Dad: Oh, fine with me, fine with me. . . .

[**Katie** *goes*]

Dad: As for you and your little problems, kids, you can all piss off; I've got a date in the garden.

Scene: **The garden.**   **Dad** *fiddles with the plants.* **Katie** *enters.*

Katie: I love all the greenery you have round the house.

Dad: Have to make the most of the available space. Even the bathroom has water lilies.

Katie: You have green fingers.

Dad: You need something you can call your very own. . . .

Katie: I'm sure you have a great deal you call your complete own.

Dad: When do you go off?

Katie: Tomorrow.

Dad: I've hardly had a chance to speak to you in the general torrent of words.

Katie: You didn't miss much.

Dad: Where are you going for the rest of your holiday?

Katie: Switzerland.

Dad: Mum there?

Katie: No, Dad. Mum's in Spain.

Dad: I'd heard you were a divided family, but that's luxury.

Katie: Not quite luxury. Mum's drinking herself to death in the Benidorm.

Dad: Bad as that?

Katie: Oh yes. She cracked when Dad left. At first she looked as though she was being unbending; then we realized it was brittleness.

Dad: Aren't you going to see her?

Katie: I couldn't bear it.

Dad: That's a tough line, seeing as she's your mother.

Katie: What they make of their own life is *their* affair. But I'm not going to suffer with them. If they choose the bottle and general deterioration, good luck to them.

Dad: A hard approach.

Katie: They didn't consult *me* when they smashed the family unit so I don't want their story now.

Dad: Then what is the choice between Spain and Switzerland?

Katie: Dad provides more fun and luxury.

Dad: Hah, he's not deteriorating?

Katie: Oh no, he's living in great comfort. Part of his grand design. He was a little uphost you know. He drove a coach for years but then started taking European tours and got ideas above his station. I suppose he was attractive to elderly widows, and always randy and ambitious. The first rich American lady to go for him found him in a state of surrender.

Dad: Hi, I thought children didn't speak of their parents that way?

Katie: They don't in happy families; it's only when it falls to bits you're allowed to examine the fragments.

Dad: Tell me, how did it affect you?

Katie: I was only thirteen at the time; it forced me to grow up.

Dad: You were also forced to watch the effect it had on them.

Katie: That, as I say, was their business. I was not a specialist in either alcoholism or nervous eczema.

Dad: Don't you go and see your mother?

Katie: I send her postcards. They're easier to cry over with the whisky.

Dad: A frightening analysis from a young'un. What do you think of us?

Katie: I think you're a happy family.

Dad: Do you envy us?

Katie: No, I'd rather be a friend of a happy family than belong to one.

Dad: Why?

Katie: Because in the happiest families I smell burnt sacrifice.

[*Enter* **Ian** *with a motor-cycle magazine*]

Ian: Dad, some fairies have been doodling in my bike magazine.

Dad: Oh, have they?

Ian: Look, underlining 'Second-hand Suzuki for Sale, as new,' and here; 'Good scrambler, 1976. Offers.' Who can it be, Dad? Making offers and defacing the adverts?

Dad: I wonder.

Ian: And my birthday coming up, what a coincidence.

Dad: Amazing.

Ian: You can have my cards for your scrapbook.

Dad: More thrills.

Ian: I'll buy you a tube of glue, what's your favourite?

Dad: UHU.

Ian: You shall have more than you can use.

Dad: Don't spoil me, by nature I'm economical.

Ian: And Dad.

Dad: Yes, my son?

Ian: You can give us a tune on your guitar after tea.

Dad: You really mean you'll lend me your ears?

Ian: I'll put up your music stand in person.

Dad: I'll rehearse my party piece.

[*Enter* **Wendy**; *looking wistful*]

Katie: Hello. You got back then?

Wendy: Yeah.

Ian: Been far?

Wendy: About.

Ian: Waitrose's?

Wendy: Bit.

Ian: Go down the High Street?

Wendy: Hmm, strolled a while.

Ian: Park.

Wendy: You know.

Dad: I've never been able to attain this level of question and answer that you children have with one another. Wendy, where have you been, for God's sake?

Wendy: When it's any of your business, Dad, I'll come and tell you.

Dad: What if I'm no longer interested?

Wendy: That'll be the day.

[*Enter* **Mum**]

Mum: Well, I can do no more. If she doesn't like us now she never will.

Dad: I didn't know it was a culinary display.

Mum: You know what Kirby is like. Don't laugh when you see the cakes in their full confection.

Dad: Shouldn't she have an honest presentation, like our twenty years of scones and jam?

Mum: There'll be enough of them next week.

Wendy: When Katie's gone?

Mum: I didn't mean that. We've put on no graces for Katie, have we, love?

Katie: Not that I've noticed.

Dad: We reserve the titbits to snare those who might marry into the family.

Mum: You're welcome to come back any time, Kate, scones and all.

Katie: Good.

Mum: And if Kirby's girl comes back a second time it'll be scones for her.

Dad: I was hoping it will be wedding bells and *out*.

Mum: We don't want any of that talk.

Wendy: I think Dad's trying to get rid of us.

Ian: You can buy me off any time, Dad.

Dad: When you leave I'll be able to afford to keep a racehorse.

[*Enter* **Kirby**]

Kirby: I'm going to fetch Judy now. Everything OK?

Mum: Yes, Kirby, fine.

Dad: All standing by for action stations.

Kirby: And I hope you're going to get dressed, Dad.

Dad: Yes, son, how do you want me?

[**Kirby** *goes*]

I'll have to use my initiative.

Scene: **The living room.** *All are present except* **Kirby** *and* **Dad**.

Ian: Fancy Kirby getting engaged.

Wendy: Must we just *sit* in wait for the girl? We're like an ambush.

Mum: Well, do something. Dance on the stairs if you like.

Wendy: She'll think she's walked into a trap.

Mum: Then *do* something, we don't know anything about engagements.

Wendy: They are more your era.

Mum: Well they missed Dad and I out . . . we weren't engaged.

Ian: Just flung together.

Mum: I wonder what sort of girl she is?

Ian: Short girl, good figure, raven black hair, pouting lips.

Wendy: What have *you* been reading?

Mum: He's been looking at photographs.

Ian: I haven't. I've seen her. I know her.

Mum: You *know* her!

Ian: Yeah, met her many a time.

Mum: Where, when?

Ian: Shall I take those questions chronologically?

Mum: Oh, get on with it.

Ian: Do you know those Saturday mornings I worked in the Do It Yourself shop to buy my miniature billiard table? He used to bring her in there.

Mum: What on earth for?

Ian: He was helping her father about the home.

Mum: God, you better not let our Dad hear that. Kirby never lifts a finger in this house.

Ian: He thinks this house isn't worth lifting a finger for.

Mum: Then her house must be spick and span if he rolls his sleeves up there.

Wendy: You know Kirby's demon energy.

Ian: Her dad is house-proud.

Mum: So is your dad; he's quite a hand when he puts his mind to it.

Wendy: Tends to be seasonal.

Katie: I think your father is more people-proud than house-proud.

Mum: Now that's a nice thing to say. He'd like that. Perhaps you could say it to his face.

Katie: I think I've implied it.

Wendy: He quite likes things said behind his back, it makes him feel important.

Mum: Not too much behind his back, miss. . . .

[*Enter* **Dad** *in a suit*]

Dad: No sign of the maiden?

Mum: You look very smart.

Dad: In a state of emergency the armour is brought out of the mothballs.

Wendy: You look very dishy, Dad.

Dad: Please don't expose yourself. Your vulnerability may be seized upon by others.

Wendy: What do you think of this spruced up edition, Katie?

Katie: I like him best sloppy.

Ian: We're talking about his clothes. Mum I'm starving. Can't I go in and have a chocolate flake or one of those custard creams?

Mum: You cannot.

Wendy: Remove one and it spoils the arrangement.

Dad: I must say I glanced at the displayed confectionery as I passed and I have to comment that an occasion brings out the artistry of your pastry.

Mum: Katie helped.

Katie: In a modest capacity.

Mum: You lent some nice touches, I must say, some nice touches.

Dad: Katie, may I say on behalf of my mute children that you have lent some nice touches to this home since you arrived.

Katie: Thank you.

Dad: I think you'll make someone a nice wife.

Wendy: That'll be some man, she's been through half the College already. . . .

[*Pause*]

Mum: That's them!

Dad: Yes, I heard the brakes slam on. Kirby costs me a fortune in remoulds.

Ian: Hurry up Judy . . . this is Mum, Dad, Katie, Wendy, me, food, now eat. Perhaps we could say the Lord's Prayer. 'For Judy's arrival may we all be thankful.'

Mum: Behave yourself and don't act the fool.

Ian: And let Dad steal the show? Never.

[*Enter* **Kirby** *with* **Judy**, *a pretty girl but dead common*]

Kirby: Hi, Mum, this is Judy.

Mum: Hello, my pet. You're late.

Judy: We've been to the Ice Cream Parlour.

Mum: But the tea's all laid.

Kirby: That's all right, Mum, pre-family celebration.

Ian: We're starving.

Kirby: We're not, you'll have to wait.

Mum: Settle your nerves, did it?

Judy: I'm not nervous.

Mum: You better introduce Judy to the family, then, Kirby.

Kirby: Oh, its OK.

Mum: It isn't OK. She can't just find people out for herself.

Wendy: The presentation at court seems essential, Kirby.

Kirby: That's our Wendy and her friend Katie.

Judy: I saw you in the High Street looking in.

Wendy: Looking in where?

Judy: Stylus; I'm an apprentice hairdresser.

Katie: We did peep under the driers. Were you styling?

Judy: No, I was on the sterilizer. I noticed your hair though. It's nice.

Mum: How do you like being an apprentice hairdresser?

Judy: All right.

[*All this time **Ian** has been pointing to himself, cavorting about, brushing his hair and other such nonsense*]

Kirby: Ian, don't be so stupid, trying to attract attention.

Ian: Sorry, I thought I'd gone unnoticed.

Kirby: You know this clown, Judy?

Judy: Hi, Ian.

Ian: Madam, this is our humble home, enjoy the masquerade but don't spit on the sawdust.

Kirby: Oh, and this is Dad.

Ian: Our old faithful retainer in the corner.

Dad: Welcome, my dear. Don't be shy amidst all this.

Judy: I'm not.

Dad: I hope that's a compliment to our friendly domain.

Judy: Yes. Smashing.

Kirby: I see Dad's gone the full suit job?

Dad: My humble compliment to your guest.

Ian: He is wearing the full formal cut.

Wendy: Sweating at the neckband beneath the decorum.

Dad: Ah, have I made an error of etiquette? Correct me if I'm wrong.

Kirby: Look around you, Dad.

Wendy: At what the inset are wearing.

Ian: I think you were badly advised by Moss Bros.

Dad: Just put it down to my lack of taste. I'll go and hunt out my bermuda shorts. . . .

[*He goes*]

Mum: Duncan, don't bother with . . . now look what you've done.

Kirby: We haven't done anything.

Ian: Dad's OK. Water off a duck's back.

Wendy: Don't take any notice of Dad.

Judy: I'm not.

Mum: You're not hungry yet, Judy?

Judy: No.

Katie: How long have you been at Stylus, Judy?

Judy: Since I was sixteen.

Mum: Oh yes, how long is that?

Judy: Three months.

Mum: You were lucky to get an apprenticeship.

Judy: Me mum got me in.

Katie: Let's hope our Mums can get us in somewhere; teaching jobs are desperately short.

Judy: Me mum couldn't get me in teaching.

Mum: How did she get you in hairdressing? Was she in the trade?

Judy: No. In the shop. She was a good customer.

Mum: Has her hair done regularly?

Judy: She keeps herself well.

Kirby: You should see her mum, very glamorous mum with her full bouffant.

Mum: I must try it.

Kirby: She's younger than you.

Judy: She isn't.

Kirby: Isn't she? But she's all sort of. . . .

[*Enter* **Dad**, *changed*]

Ian: Quick-change-artist Houdini has arrived.

Dad: Will this do? Any further requirements?

Kirby: Suit yourself, Dad.

Dad: Son, don't challenge fate.

Kirby: That's OK.

Dad: This is what I was wearing this morning when you asked me to change for this afternoon.

Wendy: Children don't notice what dads wear.

Dad: Except the mask of ordinariness; remove that and there is uproar.

Ian: What about tea, Judy?

Mum: Well, they've been out. . . .

Judy: Don't hold back for me, I can still eat.

Mum: What did you have at the'ice cream parlour?

Judy: I didn't have too much but he stuffed himself.

Wendy: He never stops. We thought we had mice under the fridge but it was his nocturnal wanderings.

Mum: We're not worried about *him*, what did *you* have?

Judy: A Knickerbocker Glory.

Dad: So, the timing of tea has to coincide with the digestive speed of a Knickerbocker.

Wendy: I hope you're not going to be aggressive, Dad.

Dad: I hope not too, the house might fall down.

Judy: Honest, you can eat 11 you want to.

Dad: But, my dear, it isn't *us* who are celebrating being engaged, it's *you*.

Mum: There's no hurry, we can talk.

Dad: How about a game of Scrabble?

Kirby: Scrabble. Dad, grow up. Scrabble, he plays Scrabble, Judy.

Judy: Smashing. I play with my Dad.

Kirby: That's different, that's in winter.

Dad: We've passed the midsummer solstice.

Kirby: No Scrabble, Dad, thanks.

Ian: You may dismiss.

Wendy: Poor Dad, never right.

Dad: Yet again.

Mum: What does your Dad do, Judy?

Judy: He stays in a lot.

Kirby: He does a lot about the house, Dad.

Dad: A showpiece? I'd like to see it. Where do you live Judy?

Judy: Rownhams Place.

Dad: That's the big council estate.

Judy: Yes.

Dad: No wonder he's house-proud, he has servants.

Kirby: Careful what you say, Dad.

Dad: I'm choosing my words *as carefully* as a printsetter.

Wendy: Dad's our only employee. . . .

Ian: And he's retiring soon.

Wendy: We'll care for him though, won't we, sit him in the corner and feed him slops.

Dad: What's your dad's job, Judy?

Kirby: I wish you'd mind your own business, Dad.

Dad: Let's rephrase that. 'I am an insurance collector, I wonder what your father does for a living?'

Judy: He doesn't. He's on the Social.

Mum: Ill health.

Judy: No. Mum works.

Dad: How can she if Dad's drawing Social?

Judy: It's part-time work.

Dad: Nevertheless, it's work.

Judy: Well, he still draws the Social.

Dad: You mean she doesn't declare her earnings.

Kirby: Dad, this isn't an inquisition.

Dad: Son, I've changed dress to suit your requirements; if you'd like me to suit your verbal requirements would you furnish me with a questionnaire?

Kirby: She isn't here to be cross-examined.

Dad: I'm not *au fait* with hairdressing and Knickerbocker Glories so I'll leave the floor open.

Ian: You could do us all a favour and keep quiet, Dad.

Mum: Should we go in for tea?

Dad: Don't make the girl uncomfortable.

Kirby: It's *you* who's done that.

Judy: He hasn't. I'm fine.

Dad: Thank you, dear, I was about to be gagged in my own house.

Wendy: Nobody could gag you, Dad.

Dad: Oh, but you can, very effectively.

Ian: You're like a running tap.

Dad: That running tap is just the water spout, the oil is underneath.

Kirby: [*With final sneer*] Don't try and tell us *you* have deeper layers.

Mum: Kirby, there was no need for that remark.

Kirby: Well, if he is going to pretend to hidden depths.

Dad: Yes. I'm afraid he is. Very hidden, very deep. Are you kids so *selfish* that you think my only life is the life *you* see? Have you no consideration or imagination to take you beyond my slippers and armchair? Do you think my only responses are to children? My only reactions superficial? Am I just the hand that feeds you and consoles you? Am I merely a mouth that says, 'Be strong, my sons,' 'Wipe your eyes, my daughter' and 'Come to Daddy all'? I tell you these are the trivia of my life; have been for twenty years. A fabric that was there to re-assure you all and give you confidence. Well you've grown up now, all of you. If my small mindedness and fatherly pettiness has been a comfort and amusement to you, take your last dose. Because now I am beyond pretence and the fatherly gesture. Kirby, your selfishness appalls me; you scoop everything into your all-devouring gut from scrap metal to Mum's devotion and jam tarts. Wendy, you are wallowing in your own immature indulgence. Falling in love with old men and titillating yourself with suspicions of incest. Please get a boyfriend and grow up. And Ian, if you want to be a clown for God's sake get a new mask because your natural one is so *patently unfunny*. Now, my chickens, if I haven't over-clipped your wings, prepare to fly.

Kirby: Thanks for a lovely party, Dad, you chose your moment.

Mum: Can we all make an apologetic gesture at the tea?

Wendy: Yes. Bring Judy in.

Kirby: If she wants to, after that.

Judy: I want to, yes. I want to.

Mum: Come along all then. . . .

Ian: Dad, if there's a banana-skin on my way I promise not to slip on it.

Dad: Good, you might have broken your neck.

Wendy: Dad, I was going to tell you.

Dad: You've told me . . . quarterly for the last five years.

[*They file out.* **Katie** *stays*]

Dad: Can you smell anything?

Katie: No.

Dad: It's a breath of fresh air that's been threatening to blow since the nursery days.

Katie: It's very invigorating.

Dad: I hope it's gone into every recess.

Katie: I think it has. There's only one thing you missed out.

Dad: Yes?

Katie: You said there was a fabric that hid your real life and feelings. But you didn't give them a peep behind it.

Dad: No.

Katie: Was it bluff? Or truth?

Dad: Hah, such truth. You see, what those kids make themselves blind to is the fact that family life is the emotional shallow-end of my existence. It is ice lollies compared to the fruits of passion. Dirty nappies compared to tear-stained pillows. Exam results to questions of life and death. Playthings to real things. I am an insurance collector. For twenty years I have been taken into people's homes, into their problems, sometimes into their hearts, and there I spend most of my life. My real life that these kids know not one jot of. I am involved. Believe me, so involved outside of marriage. I feel, feel so deeply behind those other doors; and in here, I dwell, so long alone I dwell in here. [*He points to his head*] I have kept a scrapbook all of my married life; yes, Dad's much maligned gluing and scissoring book. But each item is a story to me. They all add up to a massive volume, torn tickets, cheap hotel bills, a ribbon, a label, scraps that are *my* collection of feeling. *That* is my life, not this. This is trivia.

[**Mum** *enters*]

Mum: Katie, they've put the record player on.

Katie: Oh good.

Mum: They're having quite a party.

Katie: Yes.

[*She goes*]

Dad: The record player. Music? A party, after that?

Mum: Oh, they seem quite happy now.

Dad: Don't say they've forgotten it already!

Mum: No. I think its registered. But they're taking their cue from Judy. She likes it here.

Dad: She's certainly reluctant to budge.

Mum: I think she senses it's a home for her; it seems to provide her with security, and a comfort that's lacking in her own house.

Dad: Good on us, old sport, we've done it again.

Mum: I suspect, in fact I know, there's something going on in her house to worry a youngster *like her*.

Dad: There's something going on in *our* home to worry youngsters like ours.

Mum: Yes. But we're good at hiding it . . . come on. . . .

Dad: One more time.

Mum: Yes, come on, put on a face, she needs it, poor kid. . . .

The End

Follow-up Activities

Two Men from Derby

Discussion

What facts do we know about Dick? (His age? Job? His family? Habits? Likes and dislikes, etc.?) Find the evidence in the play that proves each of your points.

How would you describe Dick? What sort of character is he?

What possible reasons are there for Dick not coming home this particular evening? Which do you think is the most likely one?

Is he selfish? How would you defend his behaviour?

Have you ever deliberately avoided 'fame' or the chance to do something different and special? What was it? Why did you behave as you did, do you think? Do you know an older person who often talks about the great things they could have done, if only they had the chance or money or freedom?

Besides football, what jobs today provide an 'escape' and comparatively easy money? Would you accept one, if it was offered you?

Do you think Dick will regret his lost opportunity?

The play is set in 1930. How does Freda's work differ from that of most housewives today? What does she lack that we now take for granted?

Which do you think is the harder — work down the pit or housework?

Do you think housework is 'woman's work'?

Should a man be 'free' to do what he likes? Should a wife be expected to 'wait' on her husband?

Improvization

Joe's and George's conversation on the bus home, in which they discuss the day's events (or, rather, non-events).

A scene in which Freda calls on Winnie (before Dick comes home) and talks about her problems and wishes.

A scene in which Dick shares his thoughts with a friend.

The conversation that might take place between Dick and Freda when he does come home. (Note that Freda's temper is subsiding as the play ends.)

A scene twenty years later in the same house: Freda and Dick discuss what might have been. Develop the scene to include their (now grown-up) son/daughter who is wondering whether to give up a safe job and move to London.

Writing

An account of a time you have turned down an opportunity.

A short story called 'The Lucky Break', in which you are offered a great opportunity. Some of your family and friends think you should accept, but others have doubts.

A further scene for the play, in which Dick arrives home.

A paragraph summarizing the points that can be made against Dick's behaviour, and another paragraph defending him.

Though there is no direct evidence in the play to prove that Dick deliberately avoids Joe and George, imagine this is the case, and write a short story describing the day from his point of view.

Loyalties

Discussion

What facts do we know about Gallahar? Do you like him? What to you think of him?

What do Onnie's parents think of him? How far are they justified in thinking the way they do?

Why is Onnie so taken with Gallahar?

Can you recount a time when you have felt a clash of loyalties — when you have, for example, found it hard to be loyal to both a good friend and to your parents? Which 'loyalty' won?

Do you think Onnie was right to tell all he knew to Wylie? What would you have done? Is 'sneaking' ever right? When?

How does Onnie feel at the very end of the play? Why?

Why isn't Gallahar angry with Onnie? Do you think Gallahar likes him? What evidence can you find, for and against your opinion?

Do you think Wylie was justified in 'tricking' Onnie?

Which do you think is the more important — truth or loyalty?

Improvization

A scene in which two parents discuss their worries about what they consider to be the unsuitable friends their teenage son or daughter is going around with. Play the scene first with both parents in agreement; then play it with one parent trying to re-assure the other.

Repeat the scene with the son or daughter present.

A conversation between Onnie and the two boys, in the interval of the concert at the town hall, in which they try to find out why Onnie is no longer a mate of Gallahar's. (Onnie is not eager to tell the truth but it is obvious that he is no longer seeing Gallahar.)

A discussion between Onnie and his parents, after the action of the play. (Remember: Onnie no longer feels loyal to Gallahar, but will not want to admit he has been in the wrong or has betrayed his former friend; the parents will not want to admit what they said to Wylie.)

A short play about two friends. Known to the other, one has been bullying (quite cruelly) a much younger child. Act out scenes, after the bullying has taken place, between the two friends; between an adult in authority (teacher, parent, police, etc.) and each of the friends; and between the friends and their parents and the parents of the child who was bullied. Experiment with different endings – the bully being betrayed by his or her friend (and the subsequent scenes); the bully being caught; or the bully admitting the 'crime' but being defended by the friend.

Writing

Wylie's official report of the incident, as you think he might have written it up.

A short story describing a day in the life of Gallahar.

A true account of a friendship you have had with an older person – someone with whom you shared a hobby or other interest.

A further scene for the play, written in dramatic form, in which Onnie's parents tell him how glad they are the friendship between Onnie and Gallahar is over. (NB. How is Onnie likely to react to his parents' pleasure?)

A story about a time you have behaved less well than you would have wished, or when you have had to admit to being in the wrong about something.

A story about the events you created in the last of the above improvizations, or about a person of your age who tries to be 'harder' than he or she is.

Wrong First Time

Discussion

Why does Penny turn Barry down? Do you think she was right to do so? Was Barry really in love with her? Will he be pleased at her decision?

How will Penny's parents react to her decision? And how will Barry's parents react?

How do Sandra and Emily change during the play?

Throughout the play, Dad explains his 'theory' about marriage. What are his main points? Is he optimistic or pessimistic? Which of his points do you agree with?

What advice to those thinking of marriage can be found in this play? Which points would you advise them to ignore?

Do you think love *is* blind? Is it a necessary basis for marriage? What else is required?

Whether you are staging the play or not, discuss how you might furnish each house to illustrate each family's character. What costume should each character wear?

Improvization

The scenes that might follow the one in which Penny turns down Barry: between *a* Penny and her parents; *b* Penny and her sisters; and *c* Barry and his parents. (NB. Think carefully of how Barry will feel in this situation — for example, he will still be loyal to Penny, though he may also feel some relief or maybe shame.)

A conversation that might take place between Penny and Barry five years later.

Conversations that might take place between Emily and Claude and Smudge and Sandra following Penny's decision, when they try to sort out their own marriages.

Scenes in which teenagers break bad news (e.g. that they are in trouble with the police, or in serious trouble at school) to their parents. Play each scene with the parents being *a* sympathetic and helpful; *b* angry and upset; and *c* each reacting in different ways.

Develop your own improvised play about how a family reacts to one of the children getting into trouble — for example, the youngest (and usually best-behaved) son getting caught shoplifting; or a normally quiet daughter losing her temper with her head teacher. (Before beginning your play, plan carefully the interests and circumstances of the various brothers and sisters, and make sure each member of the 'family' knows such facts.)

Writing

Imagine that either Penny or Barry keeps a diary during the events covered by the play. Write up that diary.

A summary of Dad's theory.

A short story about a family row you have caused in some way.

A playscript or short story based on one of your improvised scenes.

Never Right, Yet Again

Discussion

Who do you think is the more cruel — Dad to his children, or them to him? Who is the more selfish?

Are the children responsible for his outburst?

Several of the characters are very sarcastic to each other. Find examples, and discuss whether such remarks are fair or cruel.

How do people use sarcasm as a weapon?

What does each of the three children expect of his/her father? How does he differ from their view of him? Is he a good father, do you think? Do you take his side against the children? Always? Never? When?

Should parents be selfish? At all? How are children selfish?

How do you irritate your own parents?

What ideas or remarks in the play did you find surprising?

Do you think Dad in this play is typical of many fathers?

What do you think must be the greatest joys and agonies of being a parent?

Improvization

The conversations that might take place some time after Dad's outburst, between each of the children and their mother; and then the ones that might take place between each of the children and their father.

A scene in which Wendy and Katie talk about Wendy's father, or one in which Ian accuses Kirby of upsetting their father.

A scene in which a teenager tries to persuade a parent to buy an extra-expensive birthday or Christmas present, on the grounds that it will be helpful or useful in the long run. (Try playing the scene different ways — with the family hard up, with the parent able to afford the present but feeling it would be either a waste of money or a 'bad thing', or with the parent trying to lay down lots of conditions.)

Develop an improvised play about a family meal, to which the children of the family have invited (with permission) their friends. Include scenes before the meal in which the children try to tell their parents how to behave, what to say and what not to say, etc. Plan whether the parents like or disapprove of the 'guests', and consider how the guests will react to the parents, etc.

Writing

Devise a set of ten rules for children on how to care for their parents.

An account of a time you have upset or annoyed one or both of your parents, or of a time you have been embarrassed by them.

Write a poem which says thank you to your parents for the particular things they have done for you, or one in which you say sorry for the ways you might have upset them or taken them for granted.

A short story or playscript called 'The Family Meal'.